EXPLORING ARRAN'S PAST

EXPLORING ARRAN'S PAST

by
HORACE FAIRHURST

Illustrations drawn by
JEAN FORBES

KILBRANNAN PUBLISHING LIMITED

First edition published 1981.
This edition published 1982 by Kilbrannan Publishing Limited, Brodick, Isle of Arran, Scotland.

ISBN 0 907939 05 8

Fairhurst, Horace
Exploring Arran's past.
1. Arran (Strathclyde)—Antiquities
I. Title
914.14'6104858 DA880.A7

ISBN 0-907939-05-8

Printed and phototypeset on the Isle of Arran by Kilbrannan Publishing Ltd.

CONTENTS

ILLUSTRATIONS

ACKNOWLEDGEMENTS

I would like to thank the Curators of the National Museum of Antiquities of Scotland, of the Kelvingrove Museum, Glasgow, and the Committee of the Isle of Arran Heritage Museum, for permitting access to the archaeological collections so that drawings could be specially prepared for this book.

My thanks also go to Mrs. Agnes Keddie who typed the manuscript with speed and accuracy.

I am particularly grateful to the Highlands and Islands Development Board, which most generously provided a grant towards the cost of printing the first edition of this book.

H.F.

Hopefield,
Lamlash,
ARRAN.
April 1982

INTRODUCTION
The Archaeology of Arran

This small volume about the Island of Arran is intended for the residents and visitors, not for the specialist in archaeology. The island has long been famous as a training ground for geologists but although much pioneer work was undertaken here around the end of last century and the wealth of monuments was made clear in the scholarly *Book of Arran,* little further work was undertaken until recently. No museum was established to house the finds of the early excavators and all the important objects were placed in centres on the mainland. Consequently, the significance of Arran archaeologically has been underestimated except by the specialists. During the last few years Mr. Robert McLellan has published his book *The Isle of Arran* (1970) and has written the text for an official guide, *Ancient Monuments of Arran,* (HMSO 1977). Still, however, a broader and more detailed account of the archaeology seems to be needed.

This became more and more apparent while lecturing on the subject after making a home in the island on retiral in 1973. Again during 1978–80, extensive excavations in Arran, made under the auspices of the Scottish Development Department (Ancient Monuments), have provided new material and above all have opened the eyes of many people to the possibilities. An Isle of Arran Heritage Museum has been set up by a voluntary committee at Rosaburn, between Brodick and the Castle, and here again was a stimulus to me personally to gather together and extend the local information in my possession. Finally came a most valuable offer from a colleague at the University of Glasgow, Miss Jean Forbes, to draw illustrations for a book, and it has been a great pleasure to co-operate with her.

Life in this beautiful island has proved extraordinarily interesting since 1973. Numerous personal friends have come, have been escorted to sites of special interest and have left after providing valuable contacts with my former university life. Perhaps this personal contribution to Arran and its visitors may go some small way to show an appreciation of what these years have meant both to me and to my Arran-born wife.

Owing to the considerable differences which occur in the spelling of place names, the Ordnance Survey map of the Island of Arran on the scale of 1:50,000, has been taken as a guide: at least this decision will avoid confusion for the many people who use the map for reference.

1
THE ISLAND IN THE PAST

In prehistoric times and indeed down to the last two or three centuries, the people of the extreme north west fringe of Europe lived in close contact with Nature to an extent not now readily appreciated. Food was produced locally and a bad season could easily mean famine. What was possible as a way of life meant adjustment to the environment, not over a wide region, but within the local countryside. People could and did travel, but families often remained rooted to one small locality generation after generation. From the beginning the question arises as to what conditions were like in the Island of Arran in the past and in the remote past of prehistoric times. During the last few decades much research has given a clearer understanding of the problem over Britain as a whole, but even so and especially when dealing with this island in particular, a picture can still only be painted with broad strokes of the brush. It must be a diagrammatic view also, because the information comes from several fields of study and as yet we cannot make a very satisfactory blend from the specialist reports.

Perhaps we should begin with the very obvious statement to most readers that the Island of Arran lies in the wider part of the Firth of Clyde *(Fig. 1.1)*, and is not to be confused with those Aran Isles in Western Ireland made famous by a documentary film and renowned as a source of woollen knitwear. Our island is famous for its scenery and geology, and in the latter respect, it has a unique combination of features for expert study, combined with an extraordinary variety of rocks, especially the igneous.

The jagged peaks and deep glens which form such a spectacular aspect of the northern part of the island, have been developed out of an ancient mass of granite and schist *(Fig. 1.2)*. The highest area, dominated by Goat Fell *(Fig. 1.3)*, must have changed very little in the long course of time, and elevations over about 350 m. can never have been of much economic value; there is no sign of permanent settlement at any period. Stretching southwards from the high peaks is an ancient plateau of very varied rock types, where elevations above sea-level decrease from around 500 m. in the north, to about 300 m. in the south. Much of the more gently sloping ground has a cover of Boulder Clay and peat has formed extensively, but the plateau is deeply cut by steep-sided valleys such as those followed by the String and Ross roads. Now very wide areas, especially in the lower southern part of the plateau, have been covered with Forestry Commission plantations and extensions are still continuing in the more northerly

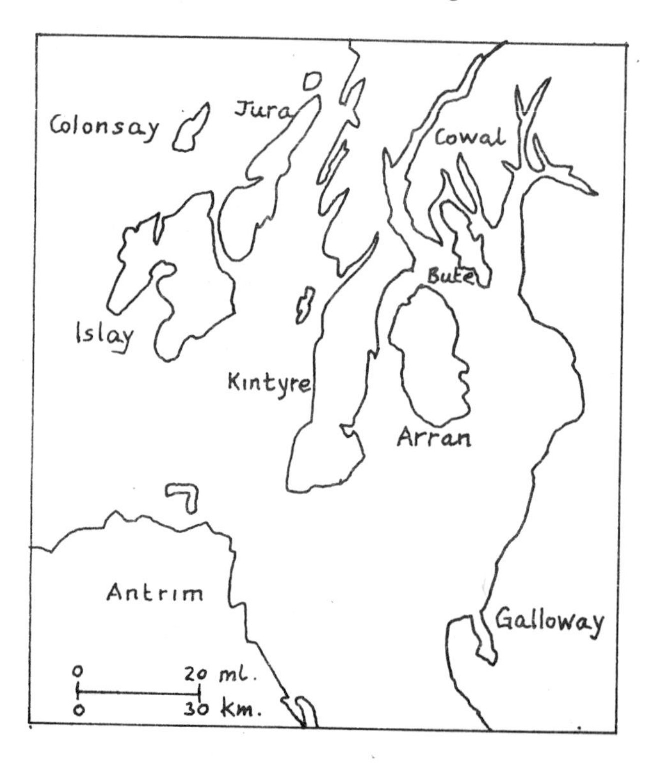

Fig. 1.1 **South West Scotland**

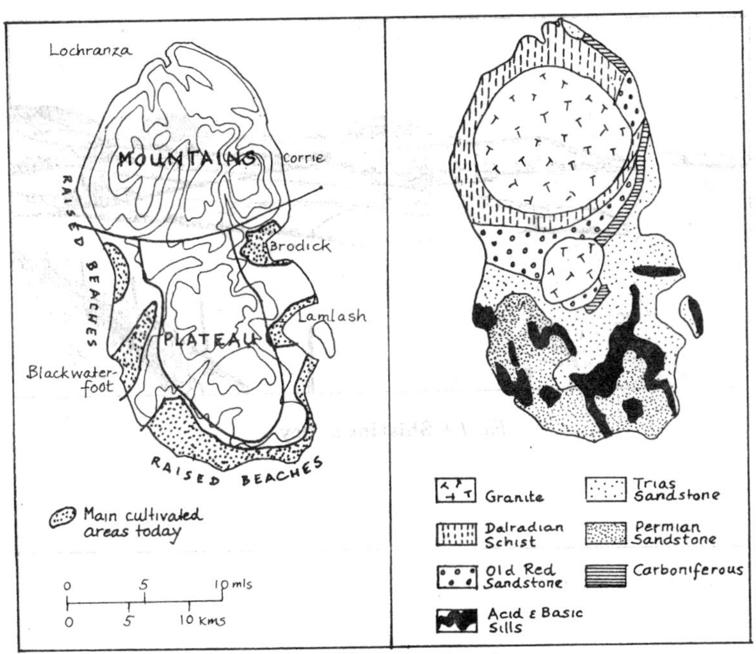

Fig. 1.2 **Land forms and geology**

Fig. 1.3 **Goat Fell and the northern peaks**

Fig. 1.4 **Shiskine valley**

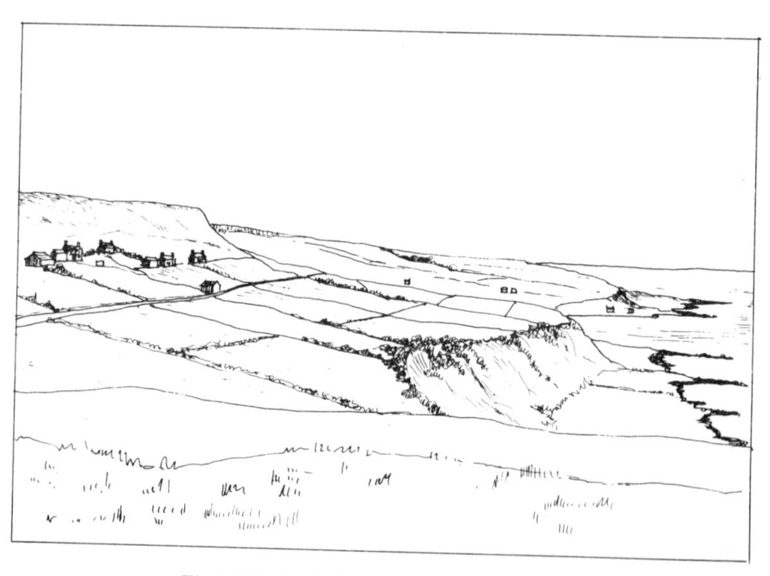

Fig. 1.5 **Raised shore line near Kildonan**

areas, even up the lower slopes of Goat Fell. Archaeological sites occasionally occur at the higher levels, as at Carn Ban or the stone circle at Aucheleffan, but most settlement has been in the sheltered glens. Here a few cairns indicate penetration on a small scale in prehistoric times, but of more importance are the remains of dry-stone houses and old field boundaries to remind us of the Clearances of the early nineteenth century.

The coastal fringe of Arran has always been of outstanding importance in the island economy. In places, and especially in the north, the area of land capable of cultivation is very narrow, or even non-existent, but the extensions of lowland around the bays on the east, at Sannox, Brodick, Lamlash and Whiting Bay, have provided attractive land from time immemorial. On the west, the broader Shiskine valley with the extensions over to Machrie Bay *(Fig. 1.4)*, form the outstanding farming area and seem to have been so since farming began in the early prehistoric period, though the low-lying flatter parts must have been marshy. Productive land also occurs in broader areas behind the southern coast as the tableland falls away to the sea. Here again on the gentler slopes where natural drainage was relatively good, we can look for evidence of settlement and cultivation lasting down to modern times.

Of special significance from the farming point of view are the soils of the "raised beaches" around the island. Formerly the sea was, at various times, at a higher level than at present, the high-tide mark rising to as much as 35 m. above that of today. The waves cut platforms in the less resistant rocks and the remnants of these now appear as a shelf of gently sloping land down to the beach. This phenomenon occurs widely around the Firth of Clyde and in Scotland generally. Most of the villages in Arran are located on this wave-cut shelf though recent developments have seen a spread to the ground above the associated line of cliffs which formerly marked the limit of the sea. The old cliff-line is particularly clear just beyond the pier at Brodick, at Whiting Bay, along the west coast from Lochranza round to Dougarie, and on the south coast around Kildonan *(Fig. 1.5)*. Dating the periods of these high sea-levels relative to the land has not proved easy, and the extent of the rock-cut shelf below the old cliffs suggests that it may have originated long ago, perhaps in inter-glacial times. The weathered sand and gravels of the higher raised beach deposits around 35 m. above sea level, belong the closing stages of the Ice Age and form the better soils, while the lower deposits of the so-called 25′ raised beach may consist of cobbles, as, for instance, along the road north of Machrie Bay.

The Ice Age was a prolonged and complex episode with a number of advances of the ice sheets separated by warmer inter-glacials. With these we are not here concerned beyond noting that Arran was thickly covered with ice in the major glacial periods. Early types of human beings had long been developing in Africa, and perhaps elsewhere, but much of north west Europe remained uninhabitable until the glaciers began finally to withdraw from about 25,000 B.C. By that time the human race was already old, but as far as we know the north of Britain had not been reached even in longer and warmer inter-glacials. The chart *(Fig. 1.6)* shows in very general terms the time scale involved, and gives comparisons with the outside world to indicate the relative stage of development in the more advanced communities of the Middle East and around the Mediterranean. The lapse of time in the prehistoric period down to Roman times, is hard to appreciate without the aid of some linear scale to show the great length of the periods involved. Arran was freed from ice not much before 8,000 B.C. and by that time, people in the Middle East were already learning to cultivate cereals and to rear sheep and goats.

The first colonists appear to have reached the island somewhere around 5,000 B.C., perhaps coming by way of the North Sea coasts from the European mainland, but more probably drifting northwards along the Atlantic fringe of the Continent. By that time, Arran was covered with a widespread forest reaching high up the mountain slopes, especially in the clefts and gullies sheltered from the wind. We know a great deal about the sequence of events in the plant colonisation of northern Britain from studies of peat deposits. Peat itself consists of plant remains which have not rotted away fully in this damp and mild climate of ours. Besides the remains of mosses, grass,

	ARRAN DATES	WORLD DATES
B. C. 5000		
	First settlers arrive	
4000		
	Megaliths (Machrie)	
		Invention of wheel
3000		
		Building of Pyramids
	Inhumation Burial	
	Stone circles	
2000		
		Beginning of Minoan civilization in Crete
	Hut circles, Tormore	Tuthankamen rules Egypt
		King David unites Israel
1000		
	Use of iron	
		Alexander the great
B. C. / A. D.		
		Roman invasion of Britain
		St. Columba's mission to Iona
	St. Molio's mission	
1000		
		Norman Conquest
		Reformation
	Clearances, Glen Sannox	
		Splitting of the atom
2000		

Fig. 1.6 **Chronological table**

sedge, heather, etc., and the roots of trees which were entombed as the peat accumulated over the long series of years, pollen grains have survived in enormous numbers in spite of their minute size. These can be isolated and identified under the microscope, species by species, and as each year a fresh rain of pollen has occurred, the botanists can trace the evolution of the vegetation by considering the frequency with which the various species appear in the successive layers of the peat.

In the closing stages of the last glaciation around 9,000 B.C. a tundra-like vegetation had managed to colonise the lowland areas; this consisted of dwarf willows, mosses and other arctic plants, some species of which still persist on the highest of the Scottish peaks. Soon came the first trees, the birches and willows, to form an open forest which would spread uphill as temperature rose in early Post-glacial times. Quite rapidly, the climate became warmer, even more so than at present, at a time when sea-level was lower relative to the land than it is now. Then followed the first arrivals of the deciduous trees, particularly the hazel and the oak, and as they spread, the birches were largely restricted to the higher ground and the poorer lowland soils. Alders, willows and marsh plants flourished on the ill-drained lowland areas which were extensive in those days before land drainage was attempted. This ancient forest was very different from the forests which have been planted in the last few decades; they consist of softwood such as larch, spruce and fir which are not native to Britain, and are close planted to grow straight timber. In the old days there was much variety in species, with differences of soil, elevation and exposure coming into play. Some fine forest trees there might well have been, but there would also be aged trees, fallen trees, shrubs and scrub, with ferns, bracken, grass and heather forming a variable undergrowth in this motley cover of the island.

About this time, between 5,500 B.C. and 3,500 B.C., sea-level rose to about 9 m. above the present, forming the lowest of the raised beaches, and penetrating inland at the head of some of the bays such as Brodick, Lamlash, Whiting Bay and at Blackwaterfoot. The small caves in the red sandstone cliffs which can be seen in places overlooking the present shore, may have provided shelter for the first human beings to arrive in Arran. They were hunters and fishers and often depended on the food which could be found at all seasons on the shore. They also gathered a variety of plants which we would scarcely deem fit for human food.

Then, at last, around 3,500 B.C., came the first farming communities bringing with them the cereal crops and stock animals, both of which had originally been domesticated in the Middle East. The hunting folk who had arrived earlier would, in all probability, mingle with the newcomers, but the numbers of either group must have been very small. The new way of life required some forest clearance for crop production, while the openings would provide grazing for stock animals. Requirements of timber and fuel would also have to be met. So far, pollen studies have been able to detect some evidence of human occupation, but the extent of the clearances is a difficult problem. The fields would be very small as there was still much reliance on hunting and gathering wild food. Moreover, the soil could be cultivated only temporarily after burning the vegetation, as the fertility would decline markedly after a few years. New ground would then have to be broken in and the old fields would be allowed to revert back to the forest to regain at least some of the old fertility.

Gradually, as time went on into the earlier Bronze Age, which lasted from about 2,200 B.C. to 1,000 B.C. approximately, population would seem to have increased to some extent, with a proportionate increase in forest clearances. The period is one of great interest to Arran, as will be discussed later, and a large number of archaeological sites have been discovered, including burials, cairns, stone circles and standing stones. We now know from the most important excavations which have been undertaken during the last few years, that small fields and habitation sites of this period were widespread on what are now the lower moorland slopes at Kilpatrick, Tor Righ Mor and around the Machrie Burn. On Machrie Moor, too, there is a most exceptional group of burial cairns and stone circles, suggesting that this locality had become one of unusual importance. However, these areas were, for the most part, overwhelmed during the next thousand years, i.e. from 1,000 B.C. onwards, by an increasingly thick mantle of peat. Soil exhaustion may have contributed to some extent, but a climatic deterioration to wetter and cooler weather is probable. Life seems to have become more difficult during the later Bronze Age and the succeeding Iron Age which began about 500 B.C. The formation of the blanket of peat would also restrict the extent of woodland on the flatter areas of the island generally, thus preserving for us the traces of the very early settlements. Machrie Moor and the lower moorland around Shiskine have remained for the most part uncultivated until the deep ploughs of the Forestry Commission have torn drainage channels through the ground preparatory to planting. Experts were called in beforehand, however, for survey and then excavation, which has yielded the very valuable evidence of the prehistoric settlement.

The story of the development of the landscape in Arran becomes even more difficult to follow from the time of climatic deterioration onward into quite late Medieval times. The archaeological record is surprisingly scanty for the island all through the Iron Age, Early Christian times and the period of the Viking attacks. Some sites we shall be able to describe later, but they throw little light on the population and the way of life in the island. There is some trace of the Vikings, but the relatively considerable number of Norse place names is not matched by any discovery of actual settlement buildings. Even later, when written records begin to throw light on the island's past, it is the history of the Church and the aristocracy which dominates the issue. Only indirect inferences can be made about the bulk of the population and the environment in which they lived. Until very recently archaeologists paid little attention to the long centuries after the Roman period, and it was tempting to think that this was the explanation for the lack of knowledge. Now, when Medieval Archaeology has become popular, a different viewpoint seems necessary and the evidence, if it exists at all, must be sought in the farmlands of today.

The sequence of events may be somewhat as follows. The desertion of the thin poor soils on the lower moorland slopes which in the past had provided some natural drainage, would seem to have involved more attention to the heavier and deeper soils in what is now the arable land of today. In time, though we do not know when, a new type of plough seems to have been coming into use, one which was better able to deal with these soils. It would have to be stronger, to cut more deeply and be capable of ridging the ground to give drainage. It would have been more expensive to maintain and would need a larger team of draught animals than the old "ard" which just furrowed the surface soil. A form of co-operative farming was evolved over the centuries, and eventually the group-tenancy farm, worked in run-rig, came into being. As will be discussed in more detail later, it involved a number of tenants who jointly maintained the plough and paid the rent. The arable land became dotted with small clusters of buildings representing the settlements of the group farms. It would follow that forest clearance in these lowland areas had become attractive. Increasingly too, with some natural growth of population as more land was won for the plough, demands for timber, fuel and charcoal burning for iron smelting, would all result in a countryside more and more sparsely wooded. The main point is that evidence for the earlier stages in this sequence must largely have been destroyed during the farming activities of many centuries, or else lies undiscovered beneath the fields, hedgerows and settlements of today.

Much of what has just been said about the distant past must be supposition, for not until the 19th century does an estate plan, preserved in the archives of Brodick Castle, throw light on the actual distribution and form of settlement. Then it is clear enough that the group farms which were still in existence, were located on what is now the arable land of today. In some cases a retreat is to be noted since those days, especially in the areas such as North Glen Sannox and Glen Scorrodale where the former tenants were evicted to make sheep runs at the time of the Clearances. What has survived of these deserted farms will need attention later. Then too, there are the very extensive plantations of the Forestry Commission which now blanket areas that were perhaps cultivated in the distant past and farmed until recently. Much might still have been discovered in these marginal areas, especially as the techniques of survey and excavation are developing rapidly. It is to be hoped that at least some carefully selected localities can be preserved for future research.

The story as we have told it for Arran in particular is, of course, applicable to much of Scotland, and especially the west, but one further aspect still calls for consideration, and that is the distinctive character of Arran as an island. Isolation is not the word to use, as the sea within the relatively sheltered Firth provided a means of contact and exchange by boat for many centuries when overland traffic was all too difficult. Looking at the ancient monuments as a whole, a very striking feature is the variety which exists and which will need constant comment. The possibility of contacts across the water must be borne in mind in this context. Kilbrannan Sound could easily be crossed to reach Argyll: Ireland is clearly visible on a good day from the south coast: eastwards the mainland from Galloway to Cowal can be seen with Bute as a stepping stone. While the variety in the monuments is notable, the actual number of sites is considerable in relation to the total area of habitable land; this is very true of the early prehistoric periods. Why it should be so is a question which the archaeologist finds difficult to answer. Perhaps the protection from sudden raids provided by the sea is, in some measure, responsible for the island becoming an attractive settlement area. A more prosaic reason is that a high proportion of land has long been rough grazing or moor, so that a high survival rate for the monuments has been possible in these areas. However, numerous as the sites undoubtedly are in Arran, our forebears, as elsewhere, have been somewhat prone to misuse the heritage from the past by re-using the stone for building material and to make dykes, roads, and even millstones. The group of stone circles on Machrie Moor is an outstanding example as they would have provided a simply magnificent assemblage had they survived intact. Nevertheless, many of the monuments have escaped sufficiently to indicate clearly and well their original form. All in all, Arran can lay claim to a unique character in terms of a combination of landscape, wealth of sites and variety of form. There is a great deal of interest to see and to enjoy, as we hope this little volume will be able to demonstrate.

2
THE EARLIEST COLONISTS

The First Hunters

At the close of the Ice Age, the extensive areas of low growing tundra vegetation on the plains of Central and Western Europe were replaced by woodland. The great herds of reindeer, mammoth, wild horse and other animals which had thrived in the old environment, vanished with the tundra. The descendants of the old stone age hunters of the Palaeolithic period, some of whom were responsible for the wonderful drawings on the walls of caves in France, Spain, and elsewhere, found themselves without the abundant meat supply of former times. They adapted by concentrating on food gathering in the forests and hunting the relatively scarce animals such as the red deer and wild cattle; fishing became very important and beach combing provided at least some food throughout the year. Tool types and living conditions changed in what is now regarded as an intermediate period between the Old Stone Age and the New, which is referred to as the Mesolithic. Nothing was known about it when *The Book of Arran* was written in the early 20th century.

Fig. 2.1 **Mesolithic flint scrapers from Auchareoch**

In fact only a very little evidence has come to light since to show that colonists reached Arran at this stage as the first arrivals, and probably only a few families were involved, crossing by boat from the west. Much more is known about these people from other sites; their stone and bone tools were found at Oban, in a cave now demolished: great shell-mounds were accumulated as refuse on the island of Oronsay; their stone tools were left behind on a raised beach at Campbeltown. The exact time of arrival in western Scotland is still a matter for research but must have been around 5,000 B.C. The last glaciers had melted several thousand years before, the forest had become fully developed and the climate was rather warmer than now. The tide reached to the higher levels of the last raised beach, the so-called 25′ (about 9 m.).

The newcomers had neither crops nor domesticated animals, except perhaps for the dog, and they knew nothing of the use of metal. Several sites where the small stone tools were chipped to shape, have been found here in Arran, notably at Auchareoch and Knockenkelly, and a collection from the latter site made largely by the local farmer, Mr. Guy Hamilton, is on view in the Arran Museum. The tools are of flint, pitchstone (which is a form of volcanic glass found at Corrygills) and of quartz *(Fig. 2.1)*. The specimens are hard to recognise as implements except by the expert, but they are, for the most part, small scrapers and borers, and points for harpoons and arrow heads. The scrapers and borers would be used in the treatment of skins for clothing, as spinning and weaving wool was as yet an unknown art. Of the actual living quarters, nothing is known; the Mesolithic people may have erected flimsy shelters which have left little or no trace for the archaeologist to recognise, but they may also have occupied some of the caves and rock shelters here in Arran. The King's Cave on the raised beach north of Blackwaterfoot might well have been occupied, but careful excavation in the future could perhaps add other sites and help to give a more precise date.

These first arrivals are of particular interest, not because of any monuments they left, but because they provided a base for future developments and their descendants became amalgamated with later colonists to contribute to the population of Arran in subsequent times.

The First Farmers

Fresh arrivals began to reach South West Scotland sometime around 4,000 B.C. and ushered in the New Stone age, the Neolithic. The name was given to the period by the early archaeologists who attached much significance to the fact that stone axe-heads were now ground and even polished to shape instead of being simply chipped *(Fig. 2.2)*. The axe was a most important tool in the Neolithic period as forest clearance had started, and the first slow faltering steps were being taken purposely to modify the natural landscape, the immensely long process which continues even now. The clearings in the forest were necessary as the newcomers were agriculturalists and stock rearers, so that hunting and food gathering from the wild were becoming less important. Flint, when obtainable, was often used for these characteristic axe-heads but tough igneous rocks were also sought and Arran, with its great variety, may well have been a source of raw material. Some axe-heads were traded far afield as for instance from the Lake District and from Antrim; examples from the latter have been found in Arran. The stone was first chipped to a rough shape and then began the laborious task of grinding the axe-head to shape with some abrasive such as sand and water. The final form was wedge-shaped, wider at the cutting edge, thickening in the middle and narrowing to a butt which seems to have been inserted into a slot, cut through a suitably shaped haft, and bound in position with thongs. The axe could be re-sharpened with further grinding, but it could rather easily split the haft. It would be quite wrong to belittle these primitive tools, however, as a well-known demonstration in Denmark showed that a moderate sized tree could be felled in under half an hour.

The Neolithic farmers came to Britain bringing with them their seed corn of wheat and barley, originally domesticated in the Middle East, while their livestock included cattle, sheep, goats and pigs. The diet, however, cannot have been very palatable by modern standards as it included wild plants which are never regarded as food now. Probably supplies were more regular than in the days of the earlier hunting folk, but famines, bad seasons and disease were always a liability; death was never far away. There is not much evidence to show what type of dwelling was in use in Britain generally and there is none from Arran. On the Continent the houses could be large enough to shelter several families and were loosely grouped into sizeable settlements. Although we know little about the domestic arrangements of the living here in Britain, a great deal has been learned from the excavation of the burial places of the dead. Particularly in Arran, the Neolithic period is one of great importance as the tombs on the island have long been well known amongst archaeologists. Over twenty sites have been discovered, which is exceptionally large for an area of this size. The investigations by Bryce at the beginning of this century as published in *The Book of Arran*, represented pioneer research in the early days of field work in Scotland.

There is much diversity amongst the tombs, but all consist of a chamber built with large slabs of stone and are often described as 'megalithic' *(Fig. 2.3)*. Considerable co-operative effort was required to drag these huge blocks from the quarry to the tomb site, probably using ropes and wooden rollers and perhaps sledges. Excavation soon showed that several and sometimes many individuals had been buried in the same tomb, the interments covering a considerable length of time. The human bones were often found in disarray as though disturbed by later burials, but rarely are the skeletons complete and it is now thought that the corpse may have been left exposed until the flesh had decayed before final burial. Offerings were often placed in the grave and some at least of the objects were purposely broken beforehand to send the 'spirit' to the underworld with its owner. These communal graves were perhaps the burial places for a group of families occupying the locality, or perhaps for the head-man's family over generations. Obviously there was an intense preoccupation with death which could never have been far away. It was necessary to placate the spirits of the dead, and fertility rites were essential for the survival of the community and to ensure success with crops and livestock. A mother-goddess was widely venerated at the time.

It is now thought possible that the early slab-built chambers

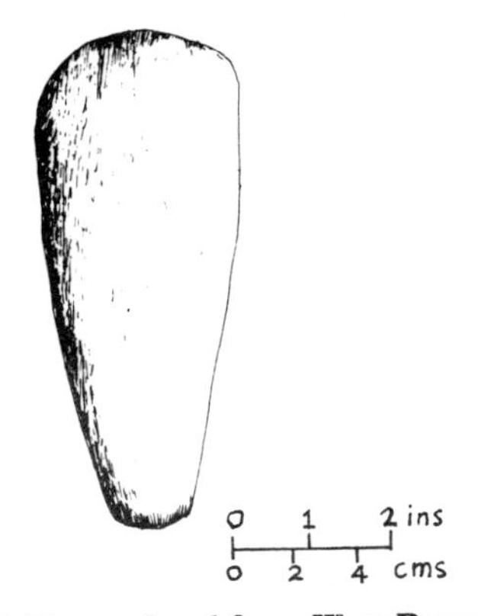

Fig. 2.2 **Neolithic axe-head from West Bennan**

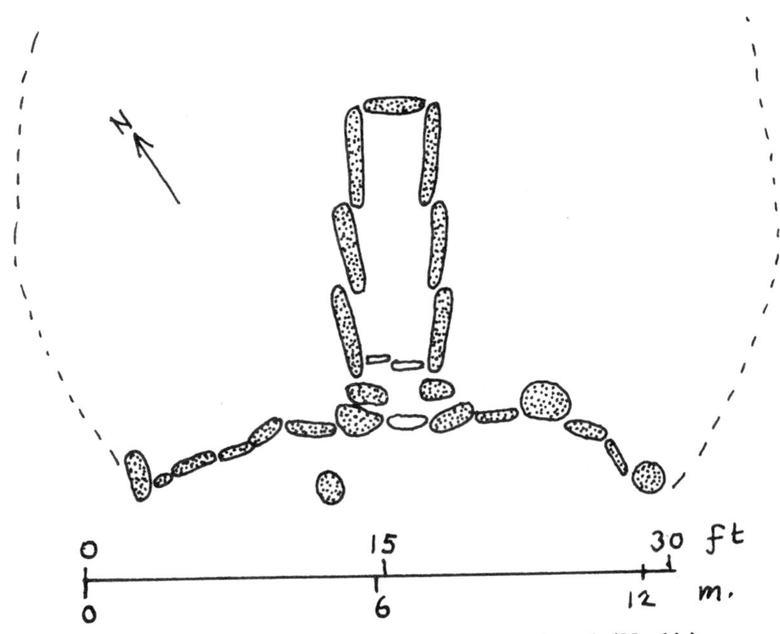

Fig. 2.3 **Forecourt area, Monamore chambered tomb (Mackie)**

resembled a large box which was covered with a capstone; there is one of these in the moor southwards from the deserted Moss Farm on Machrie Moor *(see chapter 4)*. Generally, however, several of these box-like structures were added end-to-end to form what is called a segmented gallery. Each of these compartments was separated from its neighbour by a high sill or septal stone which allowed movement along the gallery under the continuous roofing slabs. Before these were placed in position, the side slabs were brought to a level by dry-stone walling and the chamber could reach a height of 3 m. At the entrance at one end of the gallery, larger portal stones on end were erected. When the last burial had been completed, the entrance to the tomb was carefully blocked and the whole structure was covered with a great cairn of stones. This has remained largely intact at Carn Ban which lies high up on the southern part of the plateau, and measures 31 m. by 18 m. The cairns were often elongated in this way, with the tomb entrance at one end which was rather broader than the other. Sometimes, however, the cairn was round and sometimes two galleries occurred one at either end. The cairn material might be held in place by a kerb of stones round the periphery.

In what appears to have been its final form here in Arran, the chambered tomb became more complex. The cairn was provided with horn-like extensions on either side of a roughly semi-circular open space or forecourt, directly in front of the portal stones. Upright slabs were erected at the edges against the cairn material to form a monumental facade reaching out to the tips of the horns. Excavation has shown that the forecourt served a ritual purpose as small pits and traces of fire have been found, perhaps in connection with fertility rites. Side chambers might be inserted into the cairn as appears at East Bennan *(Fig 2.4)*.

All the tombs lie south of a line roughly from Sannox to Machrie, avoiding the rugged country dominated by Goat Fell. Within this favoured area the sites are scattered widely, some near the sea as at Torrylin near Lagg, and at East Bennan, while others occur much higher up in what is often Forestry Commission land, as at the Giants' Graves above Whiting Bay, or at Monamore. Carn Ban is exceptionally high at 230 m. It is noticeable that there is a marked gap in the distribution in what would appear to have been favourable land around where Brodick Castle stands, and it is likely that a cairn or cairns have been destroyed. Generally the sites occur where there is a broad view over the locality, but they rarely stand out in a very prominent position and it is to be remembered that the extensive forests of the period would have restricted visibility. While most of the

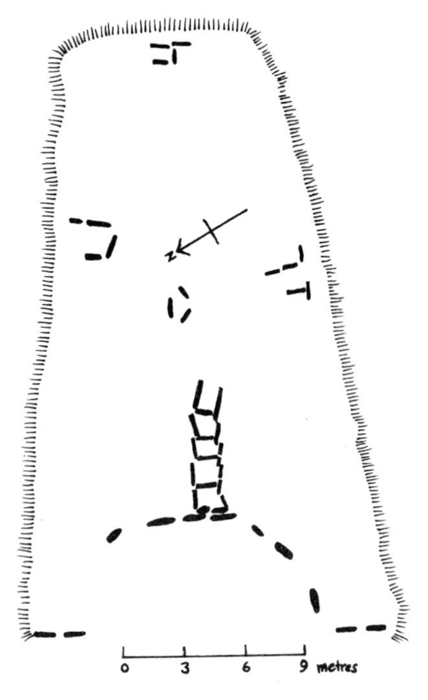

Fig. 2.4 **East Bennan cairn and chambers**

tombs are in isolation, others occur in loose groups. There are three high above Whiting Bay and there may be another three on Machrie Moor near the Moss Farm. Professor Renfrew has attempted to

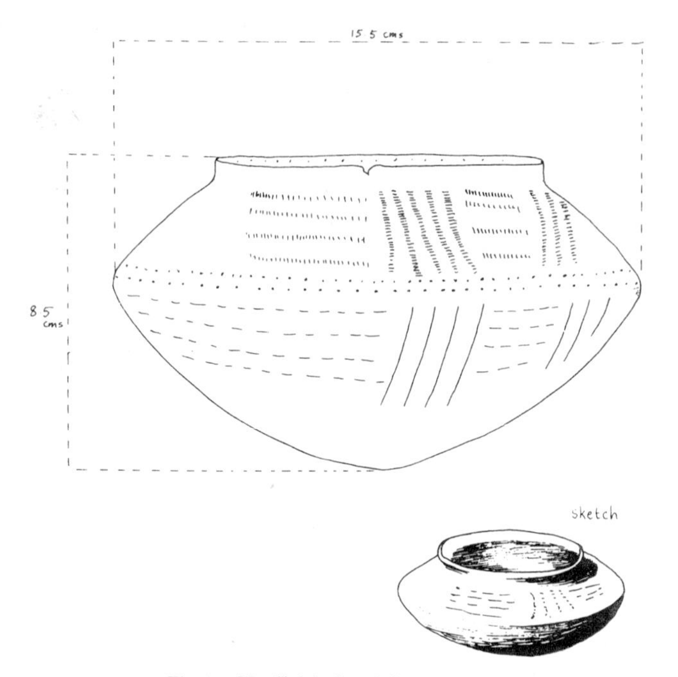

Fig. 2.5 **Neolithic bowl from Clauchog**

explain the tombs of Arran in terms of religious centres each for a district, but this does not explain the occasional grouping, nor the appearance of two on the same hillside at Dunan Beag and Dunan Mor.

During the long period since the cairns were built, they have been colonised by vegetation, the stone has spilled over the surrounding kerb, and in recent times especially there has been quarrying for stone to build field dykes, roads and buildings generally. In many cases the remnants of the chamber stand in isolation, clearly visible as the great slabs have been too heavy to move, and sometimes it is difficult to see whether there has been a cairn at all. A case in point is the site just north of the boundary fence to the farm of Torbeg on the down side of the Blackwaterfoot-Machrie road. The huge stones of the chamber rise starkly out of the moor near an old peat road into which the cairn material has apparently gone. However, a small bank where the bracken flourishes, enables the periphery and the former horns to be followed without much difficulty with the aid of an occasional surviving slab.

From the early excavations conducted by Professor Bryce, it was possible to gain some knowledge of the way of life of these Neolithic communities here in Arran. The Professor was primarily interested as an anatomist in the human bones, and concentrated effort on the chambers in the tombs, leaving the forecourt strictly alone. At the time it was hoped that comparative studies of skeletal material would throw light on the racial characteristics and hence on human history generally. Such a hope and such an approach have now been abandoned. Archaeologists are far more interested in any signs the bones and the teeth may show of disease and of the diet at the time, the main concern being to establish the way of life of the people. Then from the tombs come the remains of tools and pottery; the latter was often included in the form of bowls made by hand, commonly with a rounded bottom and some decoration *(Fig. 2.5)*. The pottery is unglazed and looks rather thick but is surprisingly good for this early period. Flint arrow heads shaped like a leaf *(Fig. 2.6)* were in use and, of course, the axe-heads. The bones of domesticated animals occur to throw light on the species reared in the period.

One curious object found at Dippin and recently presented to the Museum, would have been in use during this period or early in the next. It consists of a carved stone ball about 7 centimetres across *(Fig.2.7)*, and is one of nearly 400 which have been found in Scotland and nowhere else. They occur mainly in the area between the Tay and the Moray Firth, while the single example from Arran belongs to a widely scattered series in Western Scotland. Some are much more elaborately carved than this specimen from Dippin, but no generally satisfactory explanation can be given for their use, as no precise location has been given for the vast majority; the Dippin example is particularly valuable in this respect.

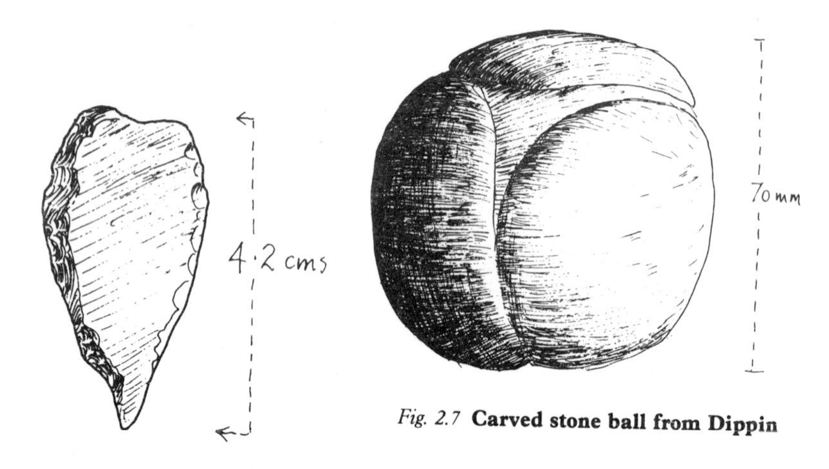

Fig. 2.7 **Carved stone ball from Dippin**

Fig. 2.6 **Arrow-head of pitchstone from Auchencairn**

More recent investigations have used techniques far in advance of those employed at the beginning of the century, and it is to be remembered that an infinitely larger amount of comparative information has become available from Europe as a whole. In 1961, Dr. MacKie re-excavated the cairn at Monamore known locally as Meallach's Grave. He concentrated effort on the untouched forecourt but cleared out the chamber for public inspection *(Fig 2.3)*. Pupils from the Arran High School later prepared a path through the Forestry Commission plantation. The excavation yielded additional finds, but also local samples of the soil were taken for submission to experts; in these days of pollen analysis, this is a normal procedure. At the same time two samples of charcoal were sent to the nuclear physicists. Modern methods allow radioactive Carbon Fourteen preserved in the charcoal to be isolated by complex processes, after which it is possible to form a general estimate of the time which has elapsed since the original carbon was formed by living plants. The two dates which became available from Monamore were 3160±110 B.C.

and 2240±110 B.C. Some adjustment is necessary before these figures are turned into calendar years and only a broad indication of the period is possible in spite of the suggestion of exact dates given by the numbers. The indications are that the cairn was in existence around or somewhat before 3,000 B.C. In fact the chambered tombs in general go further back in time than the pyramids of Egypt from which one group of archaeologists once tried to derive them.

In conclusion, one other development since the days of *The Book of Arran* may be mentioned as showing how field survey can still provide a stimulus in the interpretation of archaeological evidence. A cairn which was discovered after World War I was exceptional in that it did not conform to the gallery tombs so far described. It is located at a place called Carmahome away to the east of Kilpatrick in moorland. When it was excavated, it was found to be a very simple form of a "passage grave", that is, one with a central burial chamber approached by a passage which, in this case, was a very short one. The writer guesses that the "ring of stones" marked on the Ordnance Survey map on top of the steep slope rising above Largybeg may be another. Very well known examples of this type, when fully developed, occur in the Clava tombs east of Inverness, and the very famous Maes Howe in Orkney, though unique in many ways, can be classed as a passage grave. These tombs in Arran seem to indicate a rather different ritual practised by the builders, one which was perhaps very late and never flourished. Around the Clyde, however, it is the gallery graves which are characteristic, except in Galloway. Well known examples appear at Carnholy in Kirkcudbright, Beacharra in Kintyre and the most remarkable guardianship monuments at Kilmartin, Mid-Argyll, but there are many others for which a general guidebook on the archaeology of Scotland should be consulted.

A Brief Guide to the Chambered Tombs of Arran

In view of the very considerable interest which attaches to the tombs here in Arran, most of which are shown on the Ordnance Survey map, this short survey is appended *(See Fig.2.8 for locations)*. In particular the

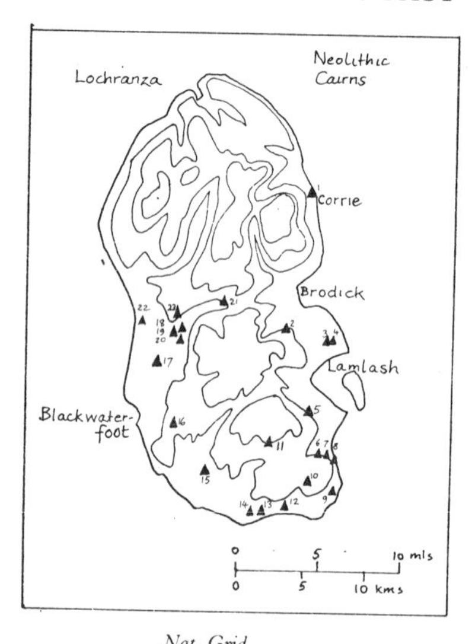

		Nat. Grid	
1.	**Sannox (ARN 1)**	*017448*	Remains of gallery
2.	**Glen Rickard (ARN 6)**	*006346*	Remains of gallery
3.	**Dunan Mor (ARN 8)**	*027332*	Remains of three chambers
4.	**Dunan Beag (ARN 7)**	*026330*	Two galleries and standing stone
5.	**Monamore (ARN 9)**	*016292*	Cairn and gallery
6.	**Torr an Loisgte**	*042248*	Horned cairn and chambers
7.	**Giants' Grave north (ARN 11)**	*043247*	Horned cairn and chambers
8.	**Giants' Grave south (ARN 19)**	*043247*	Long chamber
9.	**Dippin (ARN 12)**	*044226*	Remains of gallery
10.	**Ballymeanoch (ARN 13)**	*019234*	Badly ruined
11.	**Carn Ban (ARN 10)**	*991262*	Horned cairn
12.	**East Bennan (ARN 14)**	*994207*	Horned cairn and chambers
13.	**Torrylin (ARN 15)**	*955211*	Cairn and gallery
14.	**Clauchog limekiln (ARN 16)**	*950212*	Cairn and chamber
15.	**Sliddery (ARN 17)**	*943238*	Remains of gallery
16.	**Carmahome (ARN 18)**	*913269*	Remains of passage grave
17.	**Tormore No.1 (ARN 4)**	*903311*	Remains of horned cairn and gallery
18.	**Tormore No.2 (ARN 5)**	*906324*	Cairn with long chamber
19.	**Moss Farm road (ARN 21)**	*907324*	Remains of cairn
20.	**Moss Farm cist**	*908324*	Remains of cairn and chamber
21.	**Monyquil (ARN 2)**	*942353*	Remains of cairn, gallery and standing stone
22.	**Tormore farm (Tormore No.3) (ARN 3)**	*894324*	Remains of chamber
23.	**Machrie Water**	*903329*	Badly ruined cairn

Fig. 2.8 **Distribution of Neolithic chambered cairns**

better preserved and more accessible sites are mentioned with an indication of the salient features to look for on the ground. This list differs slightly from those given in *The Book of Arran*, or in McLellan's *Ancient Monuments of Arran*, or indeed from the authoritative and very detailed survey by Miss Henshall on *The Chambered Tombs of Scotland.* This is because fresh information in some cases has come to light very recently. Visitors are warned that some lie in enclosed fields and it is only courtesy to ask permission to pass through gates if an inspection is really necessary; most qualified archaeologists have been chased by bulls too often to wander blithely across farmland. Other sites lie where the bracken may be too high in the later tourist season to see very much of the monument.

Beginning in the north east of the island at **Sannox,** there is a delapidated gallery in the open moor behind and to the south of the village *(Grid Reference 017448)*. After a very considerable gap at the Castle park, there is another chamber at **Glenrickard** *(006346)* in Glen Cloy, but access is not easy to find.The Ordnance Survey map marks another chambered cairn at *(012347)* above **Mayish**, beyond the Mountain Rescue Post.

Next come two sites close together in the Forestry Commission plantation to the east of the Brodick—Lamlash road. The route is signposted but directions are not explicit. From the car park at the top of the hill, a track leads eastwards past the Thomson memorial and a stone circle, and continues uphill for about ten minutes walk. Dry weather is preferable as this section in particular can be very muddy. Then comes a fork and a sign pointing right, indicating a cairn and a standing stone (which most visitors fail to find). Proceeding uphill as directed with an increasingly good view over the Lamlash area, the first of the chambered tombs is reached at **Dunan Mor** *(027332)* in a commanding position on the shoulder of the hill, at an unplanted grassy patch on the right of the track. Here are the remnants of a round cairn with three separate chambers arranged radially in a most unusual pattern. It was excavated long ago but now the site is badly overgrown, which detracts from its interest; it is probably a late example. The standing stone is not here at all, but is downhill some

200 m. to the south west where there is a fine example of a chambered tomb at **Dunan Beag** *(026330) (Fig. 2.9)*. At present this is difficult and even dangerous of access because the only obvious way is down through young trees and across deep drainage ditches which are much overgrown with bracken and heather. The outline of a long cairn is vaguely traceable amid deep vegetation, with the standing stone to the north west. The chambers, one at either end, were excavated and finds

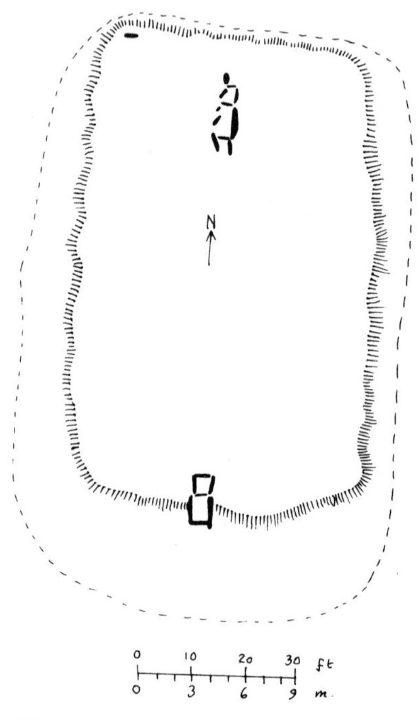

Fig. 2.9 **Dunan Beag cairn, Lamlash**

included part of a necklace made up of lignite beads, part of a Beaker pot and a Food Vessel. These indicate a usage from the Neolithic into the beginning of the Bronze Age.

Moving southwards, the next site is **Monamore** *(016292)* in the Forest. It can be reached by taking the road from the car park at the

Lamlash end. After about quarter of an hour's uphill walk, a path through the plantations is marked by a notice "Meallach's Grave"; selected by pupils from the Arran High School, it leads by several bends up to the site and over the remains of the cairn. The chamber now gives a very clear example of a segmented gallery which opens on to a façade without projecting horns *(Fig. 2.3)*.

The Giants' Graves *(043247)* lie high above Whiting Bay at about 130 m. above sea-level in a Forestry plantation. The site is signposted at the main road and the route first leads up Glenashdale before turning steeply uphill. Formerly there was a magnificent view but now the monuments lie in an open space left unplanted to allow access. The material of the first long cairn has largely gone, the side slabs of the gallery have slumped inward but the horns can be traced. At the narrow end of the cairn to the south, are the remains of a second chamber. The second cairn is small and roughly oval, and is rather difficult to recognise as separate from the first. It contains one of those single megalithic chambers like an elongated box. Yet another site has been discovered recently about a quarter of a mile (400 m,) to the north west, deep in the forest beyond the Giants' Graves and below **Torr an Loisgte** at approximately *(042248)*. It is a long horned cairn intact at one end, with a gallery and a side chamber exposed.

In the south east of the island, there is a badly ruined chamber on the side of a farm track at **Dippin** *(044226)*, while **Ballymeanoch** *(019234)* is in a Forestry plantation and is almost beyond recognition. Turning westwards, a group of better preserved monuments is reached. **East Bennan** *(994207)* is well known to archaeologists as the famous Gordon Childe selected it as a type site for the horned cairns. It lies in farmland not far from the sea cliff and immediately west of a burn. It was excavated at the beginning of the century and the gallery and forecourt are marked by slabs showing clearly above the turf *(Fig. 2.4)*. There is another tomb at the end near the burn, and two side chambers, making in all a very clear pattern. Flint arrow heads and knives were recovered during the investigations. Had it been more accessible, it would have made an alternative for guardianship to the next site at **Carn Ban** *(991262)*. This is the highest site of the island at

230 m. and is to be reached by a hard walk, first of all along the Forestry road which runs to Whiting Bay over from the main road a mile (1600 m.) east of Lagg, where there is a signpost. Then a little north of Auchareoch, it is necessary to follow a ride uphill for another mile. The site is most unusual in that the cairn, most of which survives, runs uphill and the well marked forecourt is on a distinct slope. The main chamber is largely exposed and another is known to exist at the lower end of the cairn. Excavation showed that the monument was well preserved but all trace of bones had been lost, using the techniques available then, as the soil was wet and acid.

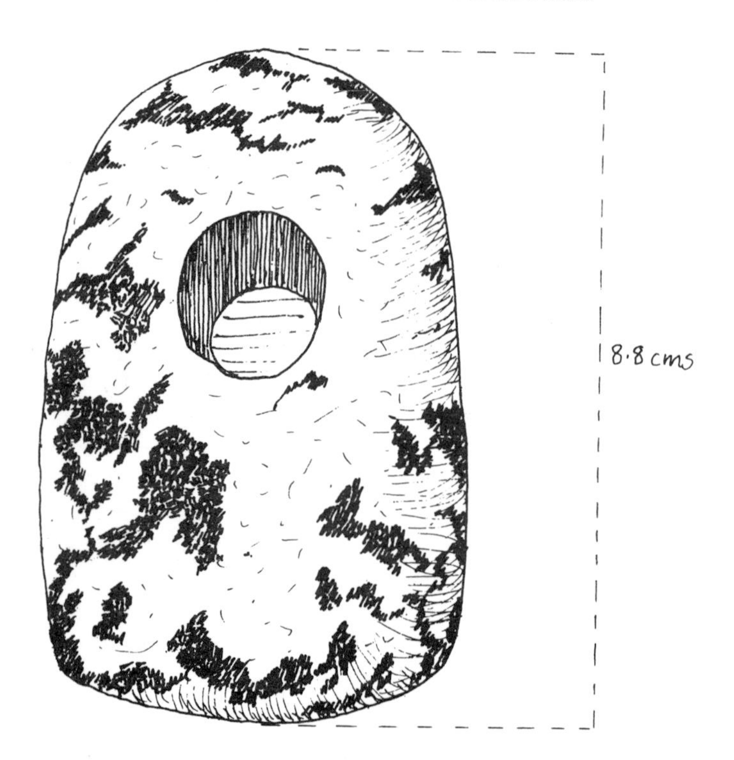

Fig. 2.10 **Mace-head of gabbro from Tormore No.1**

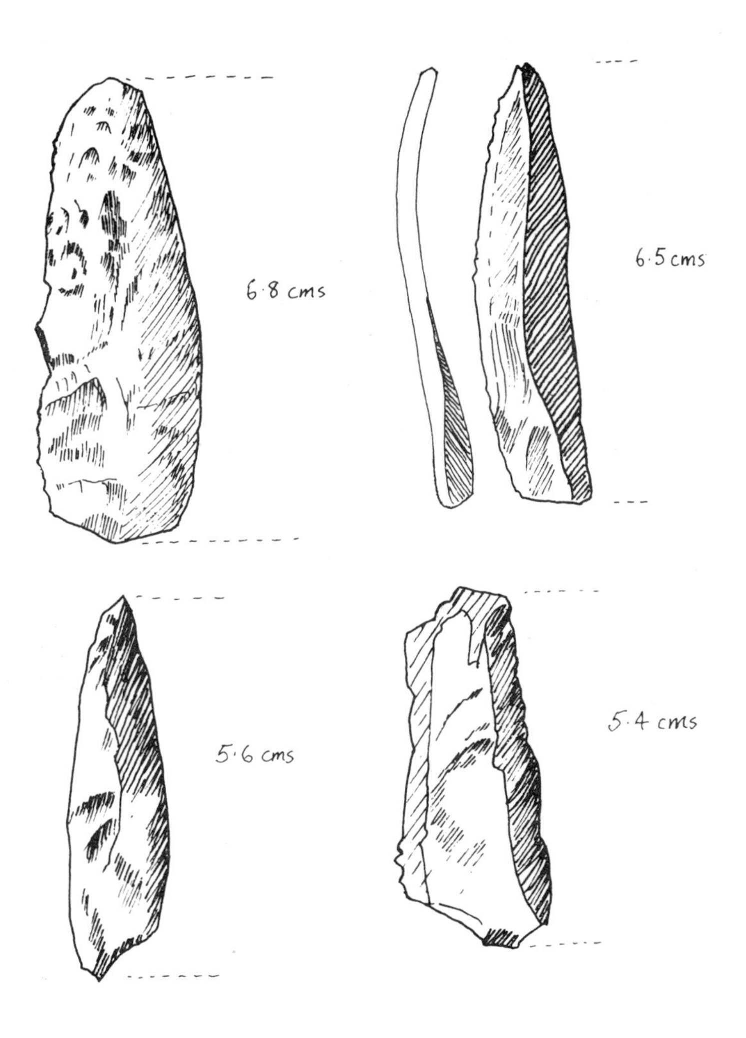

Fig. 2.11 **Flint knives from Tormore**

The chambered cairn at **Torrylin** *(955211)* is also under guardianship as an ancient monument. It is reached by a short and pleasant walk along the farm road leading south from Lagg post-office. Part of the original gallery is exposed at one end of the cairn, but the entrance has disappeared. The bones of at least six persons were found in the excavation, the skeletons being in disarray and no one complete. Across the Kilmory water is the **Clauchog Limekiln** cairn *(950212)* reached from another farm road west of Lagg. The cairn, which is oval, survives in part and there is a chamber exposed, with two enormous slabs walling one side of the two compartments; originally the roofing slabs were nearly 3 m. above ground level. In this excavation a polished axe-head was recovered and two round-bottomed pots, one of which was highly decorated *(Fig. 2.5 and there is a replica in Brodick Castle)*. There were also found the remains of no less that fourteen individuals, incomplete as before. A small cist of Bronze Age date seems to have been inserted into the cairn at a later period. To complete this group, there are the remains of a gallery at **Sliddery** *(943238)* on the other side of the Sliddery water from the farm of Bennecarrigan.

There is an enigmatic site under guardianship as an ancient monument, of which we shall hear more later, above the farm of **Kilpatrick** *(905266)*. It was formerly regarded as the site of an Early Christian monastery, but is now signposted at the road side as a dun. It is reached by a track leading uphill for about quarter of an hour, following marking poles; if dogs must be taken, please keep them under strict control. The entrance to this dun may well be the remnant of a gallery, and another cairn is suspected immediately outside. The site of the passage grave mentioned earlier at **Carmahome** *(913269)* lies far out in the moor to the east of Kilpatrick and is now sadly ruined, besides the difficulty of access.

North of Blackwaterfoot, there are three sites on the farmland of Tormore. **Tormore No.1** *(903311)*, as named in *The Book of Arran*, has been mentioned above as a horned cairn (p.23). It lies in the moor just north of the boundary fence with Torbeg, and is easily reached by a very rough track running down from the seat on the roadside at the top of the hill, above the Torbeg farm and smiddy. Finds included a beautiful polished and perforated macehead *(Fig. 2.10)* and several flint knives *(Fig.2.11)*. **Tormore No.2** *(906324)* lies across the moor northwards and is near the Moss Farm road, as described later (p.55), but is now on the wrong side of an electric fence. It is an elongated box-like structure in an oval cairn and would form a very interesting example were it less difficult to locate. Two other sites nearby, the **Moss Farm Cairn** *(907324)* and the **Moss Farm Cist** *(908324)* are again mentioned later (p.55), but both are badly ruined. **Tormore No.3** *(894324)* is a remnant built into the byre at Tormore farm. Finally, a much ruined chambered cairn has recently been recognised on the site of the cairn as shown on the Ordnance Survey map, just north of the Machrie Water *(903329)*. This local group of six sites represents a remarkable concentration, especially as it is in such close proximity to a concentration of stone circles belonging to the Early Bronze Age.

The last site to be recorded is a ruined cairn and chamber lying somewhat in isolation from the others, outside the farm buildings at **Monyquil** *(942353)*. There is a standing stone nearby.

3
A NEW WAY OF LIFE – THE BRONZE AGE

A century or two before 2,000 B.C., important changes took place in Britain and these are reflected in the archaeological record in the Island of Arran. The old practice of burial in collective tombs was abandoned everywhere in favour of individual interments, and in time circles of standing stones became common. Metal, too, began to be used, but was scarce for a long time. The earliest tools were of copper, and later 10% of tin was added to toughen the metal and make possible a better cutting edge. The use of bronze was only one aspect of the changes which were taking place, but the evidence for the first appearance of metal was easily recognised by the pioneer archaeologists early last century. The period was named the Bronze Age, and although other important developments are now known to have taken place, the old name has been retained. This is the period of the great civilisations of Egypt and Mesopotamia, of Crete and Mycenae in Greece *(see Fig. 1.6)*. The Bronze Age in the Mediterranean region lasted until around 1,000 B.C., when the Iron Age seems to have begun during very confused times. In the north west of Europe, the use of iron was much delayed and came to Scotland around 500 B.C.

In Arran the earlier Bronze Age in particular is a period of remarkable archaeological interest, as was the previous Neolithic. Stone circles and standing stones have survived in considerable numbers and they become the characteristic monuments. Several large cairns are also to be noted, while numerous individual burials have been unearthed and are still being encountered during deep ploughing operations. The number of known bronze objects is rather small but gold ornaments have been reported from several localities to add interest to the archaeological record *(Fig. 3.1)*.

In Britain generally, it has been possible to establish the fact that an invasion of people from the Continent occurred at the beginning of the Bronze Age. Excavation of burials has shown that the new element

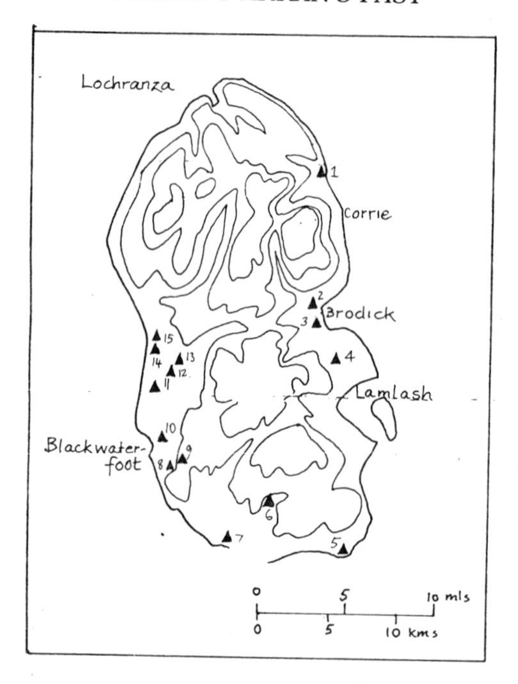

BRONZE AGE SITES

		Nat. Grid	
1.	**North Sannox**	*014467*	Cairn
2.	**Brodick old deer park**	*006374*	3 Standing stones
3.	**Brodick school**	*010367*	Standing stone
4.	**Lamlash–Brodick hill**	*018336*	Stone circle
5.	**Kildonan**	*035210*	Standing stone
6.	**Aucheleffan**	*978251*	Stone circle
7.	**Clauchog**	*950215*	Cairn
8.	**Kilpatrick**	*906261*	Field system
9.	**Kilpatrick**	*905261*	Cairn
10.	**Cairn farm**	*898282*	Cairn
11.	**Tor Righ Mor**	*896312*	Field system
12.	**Machrie moor**	*910324*	1 Standing stone and 7 stone circles
13.	**Machrie**	*901341*	Field system
14.	**Auchagallon**	*893346*	Stone circle
15.	**Auchencar**	*891364*	Standing stone

Fig. 3.1 **Distribution of Bronze Age sites**

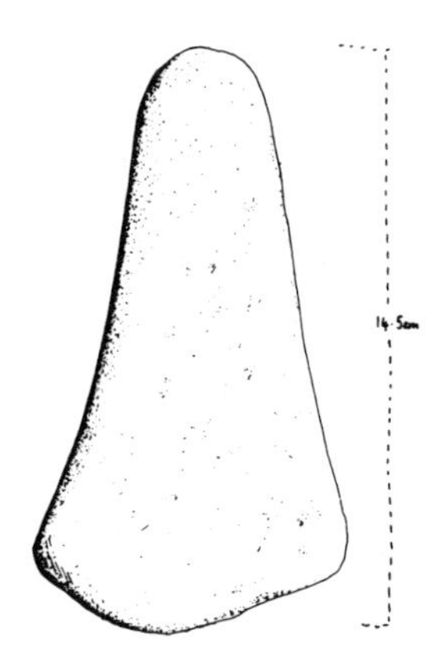

Fig. 3.2 **Flat bronze axe-head from Bennan**

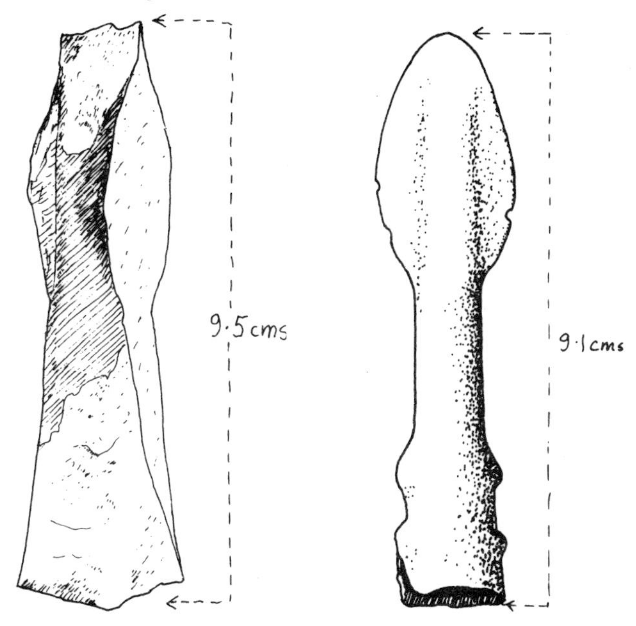

Fig. 3.3 **Flanged bronze axe-head from Ballymeanoch, Argyll**

Fig. 3.4 **Socketed spear-head from Cloined**

involved a rather tall round-headed type, recognisable by the experts from the more slender long-headed types whose remains occurred in the Neolithic tombs and so much interested Professor Bryce in the old days. In these new graves, a large pot was usually found with other personal possessions, and from its shape the invaders have been christened the Beaker Folk. Their remains are common in eastern and southern Britain, especially in Aberdeenshire. In the west, a somewhat different element appears to have been involved, suggesting that rather rare groups found their way along the Atlantic coast. The remains of one of these western beakers was recovered from the Neolithic tomb of Dunan Beag, and recently Beaker sherds have been discovered elsewhere on the island in a different context. The pottery is a hard and thin red ware, ornamented by means of a toothed stamp.

At this early stage in the Bronze Age, metal tools seem to have been too scarce to have been lost by including them as part of a dead person's equipment for the next world. Even now copper is a comparatively rare metal, though small deposits of ore worth mining in those early days occurred in Mid-Argyll, and perhaps traces were found in Arran. Tin to make the bronze was very rare indeed and the deposits in Cornwall would be very important in those times. Hence bronze was always expensive and never in great supply. Both metals, however, were easier to produce from the ore than iron and this largely explains the earlier use of copper and bronze, though deposits of iron ore were widespread. The earliest axes which were cast in simple stone moulds, were flat in shape *(Fig. 3.2)* and would be hafted in much the same way as the old stone ones; several of these flat axes have been found in Arran. Later and elsewhere than here methods were evolved of casting in clay moulds. It became possible to make axes with ridges along the edges to stiffen the blade *(Fig 3.3)*, and transversely across to prevent splitting the haft; two of these so-called 'palstaves' from West Bennan are on view in the Arran Museum. Ultimately the use of moulds in several pieces made it possible to cast a socketed axe, often ornamented, which would be mounted on the end of a knee-shaped haft. Daggers which were tanged at an early stage for mounting in the hilt, were lengthened to form swords, and later the handle was cast as

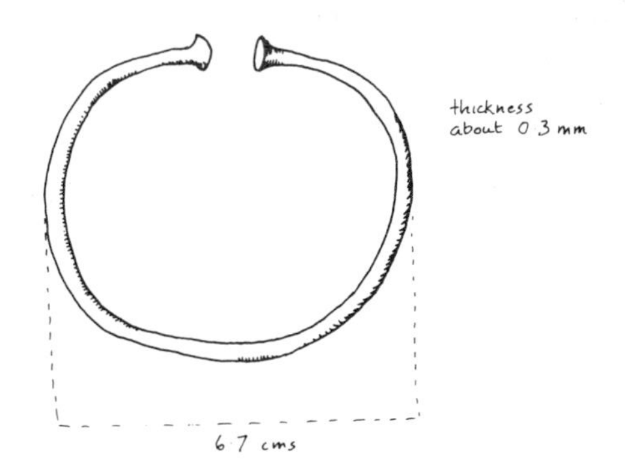

Fig. 3.5 **Gold armlet from Ormidale**

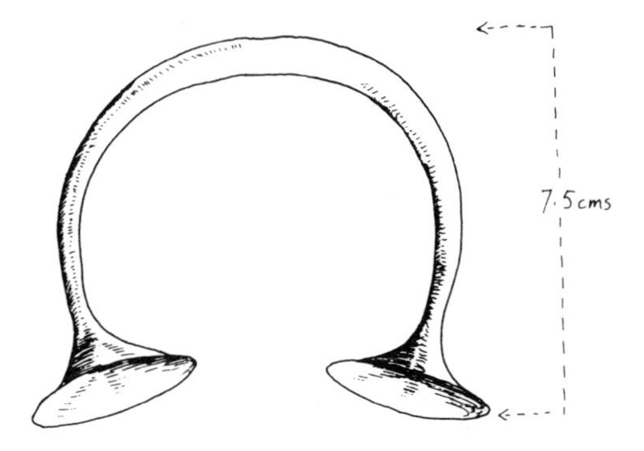

Fig. 3.6 **Gold dress fastener from Whitefarland**

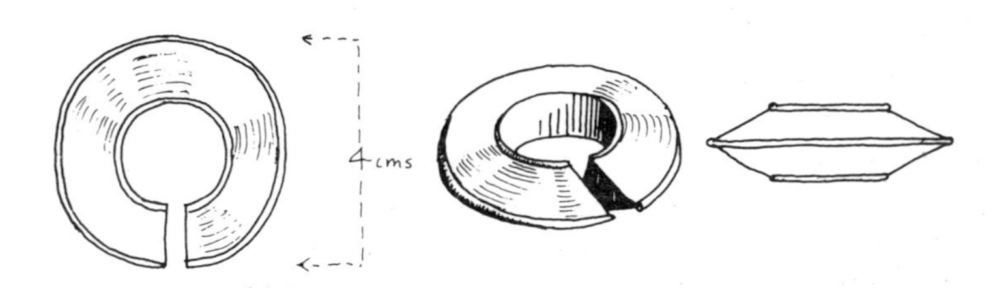

Fig. 3.7 **Gold lock-ring from Whitefarland**

an integral part of a strong leaf-shaped sword. Socketed spear heads were also evolved *(Fig 3.4)*. These were developments of the later Bronze Age, but the form of the objects, the typology, is a useful guide to the relative age, and in earlier days had to be relied upon to estimate the time for manufacture, only, of course, in general terms.

Gold also began to appear in ornaments during the Bronze Age. Ireland, in particular, developed as a great producing and exporting area. The precious metal was used at an early stage to decorate the haft of a dagger which was obtained from a cairn at Blackwaterfoot, which will be discussed later. The dagger is now in the National Museum of Antiquities in Edinburgh but is much corroded. Other objects in the form of armlets *(Fig. 3.5)* have been discovered in the island; in the same museum are four found at Ormidale, and another "penannular ring of gold" was found at South Kiscadale but was lost long ago. The finest ornaments, however, were discovered just near the road at Whitefarland on the west coast. These comprise a splendid penannular ring of solid gold *(Fig. 3.6)* with trumpet-shaped ends, which was probably a dress fastener, and a wonderful little round object made of thin plates which has been interpreted as a ring to hold in place a lock of hair *(Fig. 3.7)*. The two latter objects are preserved in the Kelvingrove Museum in Glasgow, but replicas have been presented to the Arran Museum and are on display at Rosaburn.

There is evidence now from the island here, that the people of the Bronze Age lived in circular houses which were by no means small, some of them being 9 —12 m.in diameter. The conical roof of thatch was supported by rafters resting on the surrounding wall of stone or stone and earth; further support was given by vertical posts set into the earth floor *(Fig. 3.8)*. Foundations of houses similar to this have often been recognised in the past as "hut-circles", especially in the area between Dougarie and Kilpatrick, with Machrie Moor centrally placed. Until recently and based on evidence from elsewhere, notably Sutherland, the hut circles have been attributed rather to the later period of the Iron Age, but recent excavations carried out in advance of tree planting and conducted by the Central Excavation Unit have given a different result. Careful investigation directed by John Barber

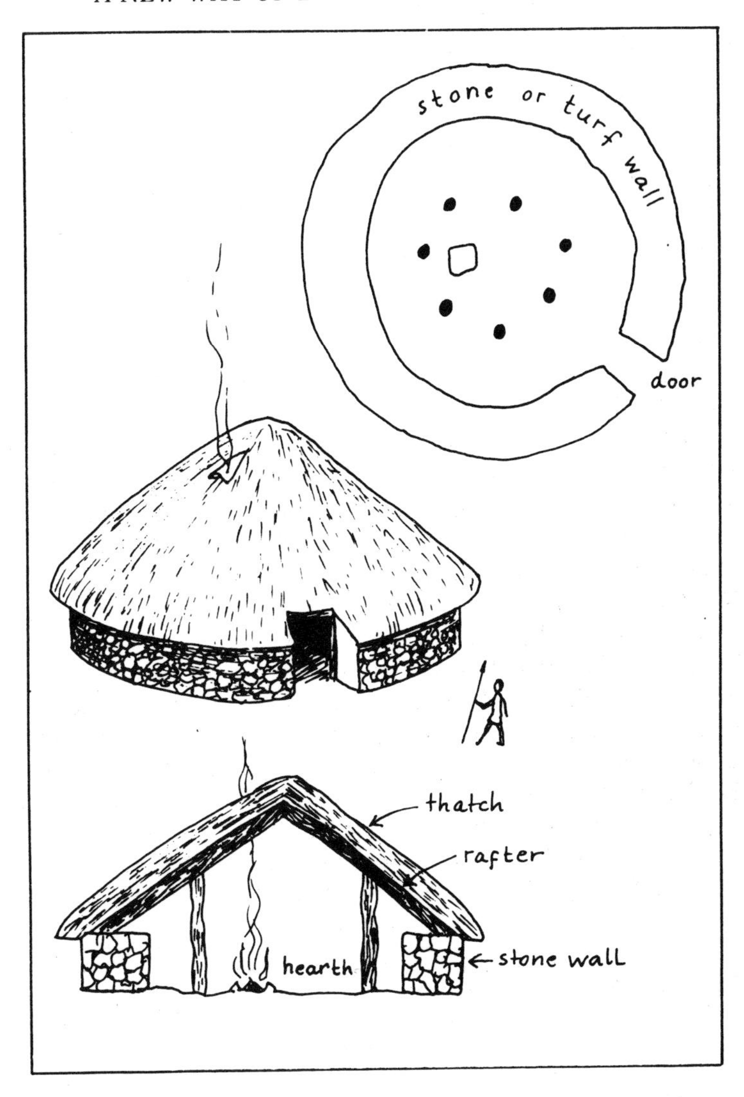

Fig. 3.8 **Reconstruction of prehistoric round-house (Fairhurst)**

at Tormore, Kilpatrick and north of Machrie farm, has placed Arran in the forefront of research in this direction; until recently, investigation of "hut circles" has been seriously neglected in Scotland.

Outside the remains of these circular houses, low banks and mounds of stones have been traced, and it is now known that the former represent the limits of small fields of the period, and the latter the heaps of stones piled together out of the way during cultivation. It has been discovered that primitive ploughs called ards were in use which broke up the top soil but did not turn over a neat furrow. Traces of both the houses and the small fields have been preserved under a mantle of peat which formed after the settlements were abandoned and which may have hastened the end. Excellent examples of "hut-circles" (which have not been excavated) can be seen when the bracken is not too high, in the moorland across the burn from the dun at Kilpatrick *(905266)*. There are three well marked rings but the low field boundaries are very difficult to recognise without the aid of an expert. Two more "hut-circles" can be found some 350 m. west of the dun in more open ground. All five were wrongly interpreted as monks' cells in *The Book of Arran.*

Apart from axe-heads and weapons of war such as spears, swords and daggers, many tools would still be made from wood, stone and bone, as in earlier periods. Metal was expensive when copper and tin were the basic constituents. Of special interest, however, were the arrow heads which were often beautifully made from flint; instead of the simple leaf-shape of Neolithic times, they were now made with projecting barbs and a tang for attachment to the shaft *(Fig. 3.10)*. These have turned up in Arran in considerable numbers.

Graves dating to the Bronze Age have been found frequently on the island and even now deep ploughing is liable to disturb one of these. Often there are no surface indications, not even a small round cairn. Other graves, however, have been found in excavating or removing really large cairns which may mark the burial of a chieftain. In general, the grave itself takes the form of a box or "cist", measuring rather more than a metre long but less in width and depth, made by setting four large slabs on end *(Fig. 3.11)*. The body was inserted in a crouched

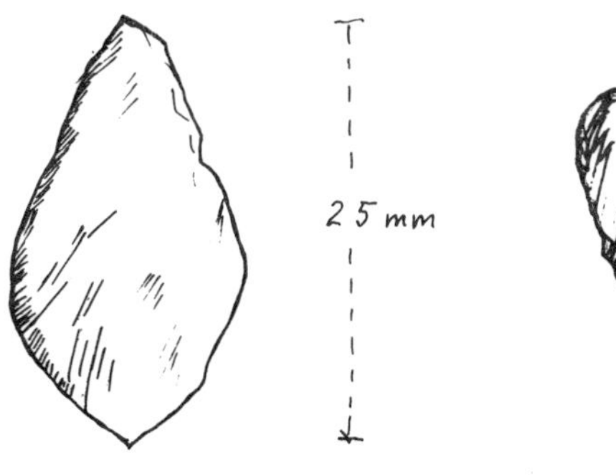

Fig. 3.9 **Leaf-shaped arrow-head of flint (Neolithic)**

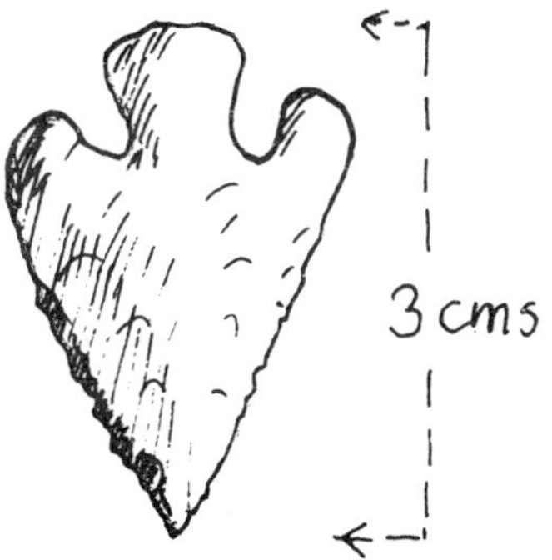

Fig. 3.10 **Barbed arrow-head of flint (Bronze Age)**

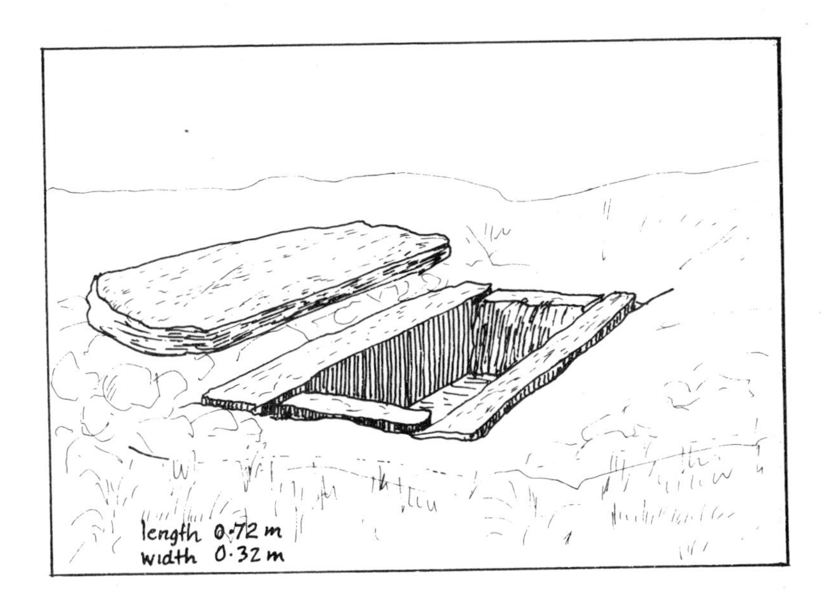

Fig. 3.11 **Cist found in the old deer park, Brodick**

Fig. 3.12 **Food vessel from old deer park cist**

position and with it there was normally a thick-walled pot, shaped rather like a plant-pot with a narrow base. It was decorated all over the outside, normally with impressions indicating that a twisted cord had been wound round and pressed into the clay before baking *(Fig. 3.12)*. The pot is thought to have contained sustenance for the journey to the next world and has been called a "Food Vessel". A large cap-stone covered the cist after the interment had been made. Later in the Bronze Age, cremation became customary, though some communities seem to have practised it before the end of the Neolithic. The incinerated bones were usually placed in a pot which was often very large and was buried mouth downwards. The decoration was also different and these pots are called "Cinerary Urns" *(Fig. 3.13)*. There is an example of one on display at the Arran Museum. The cremation burials may occur singly but often appear in groups in a cemetery, as it were. Little or nothing in the way of grave goods appear, so that the archaeologist learns less from the burials than in previous periods. The pots of the Bronze Age are thick but are usually in a very fragile condition when found, and must be handled with great care by an expert.

Many cist burials have been reported from Arran, especially in the low ground of the Brodick, Machrie and Shiskine areas. Normally on

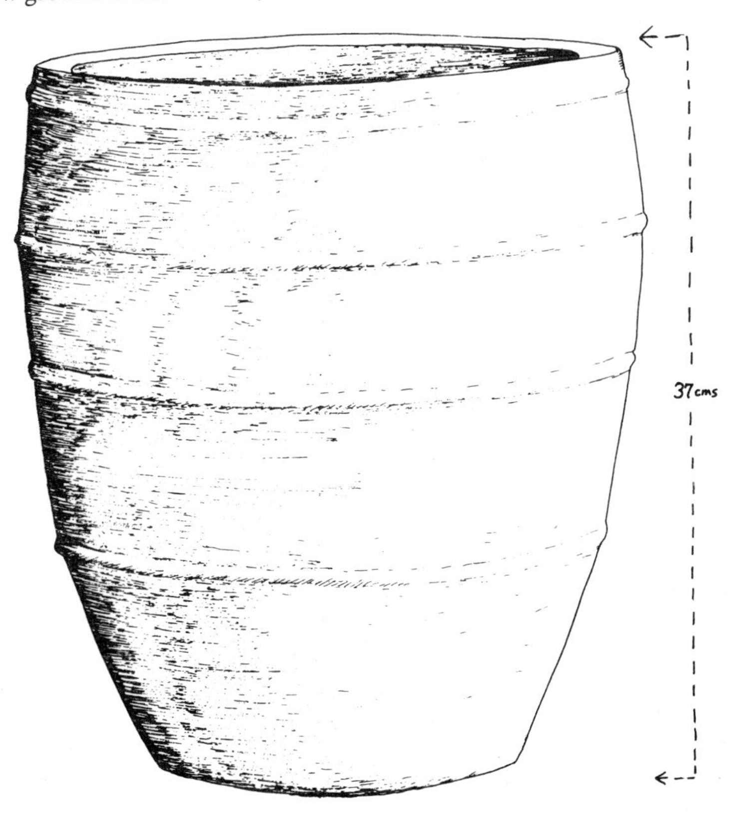

Fig. 3.13 **Cinerary urn from Shiskine**

discovery the cist has been dismantled as interfering with cultivation and rarely does anything survive to be seen at present. Recently, however, a cist was found while deep ploughing was taking place in what was formerly the deer park below Brodick Castle *(Fig. 3.11)*. After the Food Vessel had been safely removed, the cist was taken to pieces by permission of Mr. Charles Fforde, and carefully reconstructed inside the museum where it is on view. The pot is a fine example of its type but no bones whatsoever were found in what was a very neat but small cist. The site, which was not far from the main drive, is doubly interesting as it is almost precisely in line with two high standing-stones which are a prominent feature close by. A third stone stands in the field across the drive, somewhat out of line with the other two. More human remains have been found in the same field as the cist, and the Ordnance Survey 25,000 sheet covering the Brodick area, records the site of a stone circle across the Rosa Burn. Obviously this area was one of special sanctity in the earlier part of the Bronze Age and more discoveries might well be made in the vicinity.

Several of the larger cairns which have been found in the island deserve special mention. One which has survived in a readily accessible position can be seen at the car park in the picnic area at North Sannox *(014466)*. It is badly overgrown in the summer time and at first sight appears to be a featureless mound, but several slabs on end project in places. Another cairn which has been excavated recently at Kilpatrick, lies on top of the hill east of the dun *(908264 approx.)*. This proved to have been used several times over and was surrounded by a circular kerb. One of the best known examples lay on the site of the present Cairn Farm just outside Blackwaterfoot. It was described by Pennant in the eighteenth century as "stupendous" and is said to have contained a number of cists when it was demolished. More recently a large cist was discovered near the centre, in which a bronze dagger decorated with a thin band of gold was found. The great capstone seems to have been used later to house the pivot for the turn-table of a horse-engine now dismantled, but traces of the cairn appear to have survived.

Undoubtedly of outstanding interest in Arran, and for that matter in

Scotland generally, are stone circles and also the isolated standing stones. The latter may be dismissed briefly, for few sites have been thoroughly excavated and they vary enormously in age. The two in close proximity to the chambered cairns at Monyquil and Dunan Beag may belong to the Neolithic period. Some are definitely of Bronze Age date and may mark burial places. Others may be recent and it is worth recording that an imposing specimen was erected at the Nature Centre in Brodick a few years ago. Apart from the alignment of three in the old deer park which have been mentioned already, two others are well known; one stands at the roadside nearly opposite the school in Brodick, and one standing nearly 3 m. high lies in a field at Auchencar *(891364)*. All five consist of large upright slabs which show obvious signs of weathering after nearly four thousand years, but on the other hand, sometimes only a natural boulder has been used.

Over a dozen sites of stone circles are known to exist in Arran, which is a high concentration for Britain as a whole, though other even larger concentrations occur, notably in Aberdeenshire, Perthshire, the Lake District and in Northern Ireland. The island sites, however, vary very considerably both in size and appearance from the remains of two sites with huge uprights on Machrie Moor, to rough boulders on the summit of the Brodick—Lamlash hill, and from rings of 14 m. in diameter to minute "Four Posters" not much more than a metre across, as, for instance, on the Forestry road between Aucheleffan and Auchareoch. The finest single circle is that at Auchagallon, but the group of no less than six in close proximity at the west end of Machrie Moor represents a most remarkable cluster. Unfortunately, three of the latter have suffered badly during the long course of time, but the group is sufficiently important to warrant a special section later (p.53).

The great variability of the circles in Arran, most of which are marked on the Ordnance Survey map, requires some discussion, as the present monuments differ so much. One thing they nearly all have in common, and that is a splendid view over the neighbourhood, and often to the far distance; this must surely have been a factor influencing the original choice of site. Auchagallon *(893346) (Fig. 3.14)* on a hillside not far from the main road, has a view away to

Machrie Moor, over to Kintyre and on a clear day to Northern Ireland. The stones of this large circle are graded from small slabs on the east to three massive slabs to the west. One of these is closely fitted between the other two and has a relatively flat top; a cist is said to have been found within the circle. Now this type of "Recumbent Circle", as it is called from the flat topped slab, is found commonly in Aberdeenshire, Perthshire and South West Ireland. The "Four Poster" type is also found in Perthshire and somewhat similar examples occur again in South West Ireland. The Arran examples are quite minute and consist merely of four slabs set in a square, the stones being small and easily overlooked. At least three sites are known, one at Aucheleffan *(978251)*, another lies well up the Machrie Burn on a moraine *(908351)* and there is the remnant of another on the edge of a scrubby wood at the east end of Machrie Moor near the String road *(928325)*. The occurrence of both the Recumbent and the Four Poster types here in Arran seems to indicate the existence of trade routes in the Bronze Age between North East Scotland and Northern Ireland and even the South West.

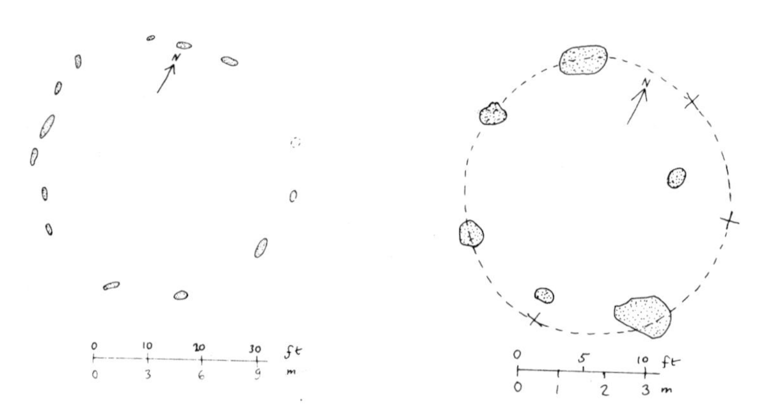

Fig. 3.14 **Stone circle at Auchagallon**

Fig. 3.15 **Stone circle summit Lamlash–Brodick road**

On top of the Brodick–Lamlash hill immediately east of the road *(018336)*, there is an incomplete ring of untrimmed boulders of which there were originally seven, with an outlier to the south some 20 m. away *(Fig. 3.15)*. There was a cist in the middle cut into the sandstone

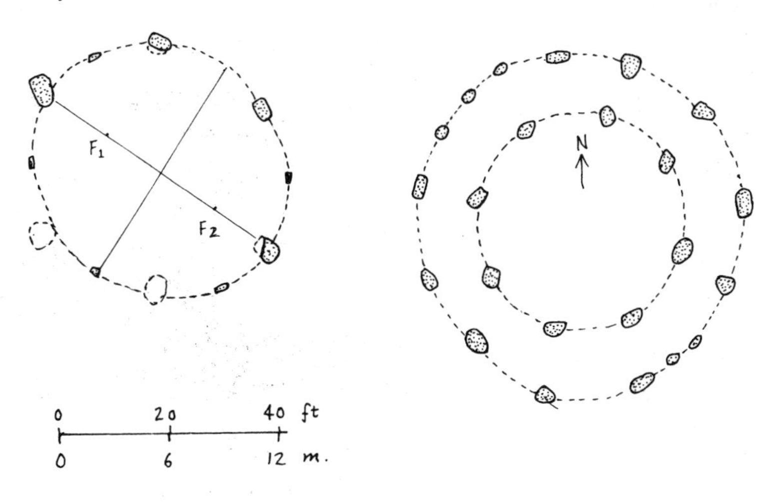

Fig. 3.16 **Stone circles at Machrie Moor (Roy, McGrail & Carmichael)**

and containing burnt bone; the magnificent view over the northern mountains is, of course, very well known. The circles with massive slabs still standing on Machrie Moor provide yet another type and the double ring of boulders is a variation unique on the island *(Fig. 3.16)*. In addition to the twelve circles visible as such, the records indicate that there were others, one across the Rosa Burn from the old deer park at Brodick, one near Drumadoon Farm, and perhaps another somewhere far out in Machrie Moor.

How the large slabs of stone were hauled into position is a constant source of wonder in this mechanical age. In fact, experiment, and also observation in other parts of the world, have shown that only a small group is needed when experience has shown the way. Rollers of tree trunks, sledges, long ropes for haulage, and long wooden levers applied in the right places can enable the stones to be dragged along and hoisted on to a ramp before being slid into holes already prepared. It is to be recalled that a good quarter of the length of vertical slabs will lie underground to ensure stability. Quarrying the slabs could be achieved by hammering wedges in the natural joints and bedding planes in the rock and then pouring water on to the wood to increase the tension. Battering the slabs to shape must have been a tedious business when only hard stone pounders could be used. None of these prosaic details, however, can possibly detract from the wonder created by these ancient circles in their stark simplicity, especially when seen in a moorland setting. Inevitably the question arises as to why all this labour should be deemed necessary.

Here is a type of question which is difficult to answer by the archaeologist whose excavations yield only material objects, and even more difficult is the explanation for the tight group on Machrie Moor. "Ritual significance" is the normal covering expression, and surely some religious motive is involved. The fact that one or more cist burials have been found normally within the circles, usually containing a Food Vessel, seems to confirm this idea of sanctity. A date in the Bronze Age is thus indicated, but some stone circles in the British Isles clearly belong to the later Neolithic period. Much controversy, however, has arisen over the question of the intentions of the builders and arguments have repeatedly been put forward that the circles served an astronomical purpose. Stonehenge has long been considered from this angle and recent studies aided with a computer, have led to what seem at first sight to be the most extravagant claims to the effect that not only could the rising and setting positions of the sun, and even the moon, be determined for the year, but that eclipses could be foretold. Stonehenge comprises a highly complex and unique series of circles, but, incidentally, neither it nor any of our circles in Arran can possible be associated with the druids; they came to the fore much later in the Iron Age. An astronomer from the University of Glasgow, Dr. Roy, has examined the circles at Machrie, but confined himself to very accurate surveys, emphasising the fact that some are not strictly circular.

In an age when writing was unknown, it is tempting to think that some circles might have been built so that the turning point of the seasons could be recognised for agricultural purposes. Undoubtedly a special orientation has often been recorded, for instance, the alignment of stones towards the rising sun on Midsummer morning, or toward the rising and setting of the moon, which, by the way, vary both during the year, over a period of nineteen years, and again over the centuries. In a most readable book entitled *Rings of Stone* (1979), Dr. Aubrey Burl puts forward a very sober view to the effect that the circles were built primarily to be used as local meeting places, and any special orientation is likely to be explained by the fact that the sun and the moon were both regarded as of great religious significance, hence the attention to rising and setting points. It is all a difficult question, giving rise to violent differences of opinion; to avoid misapprehension, my own view is one of scepticism over astronomical interpretations. An equally difficult problem seems to be the reason why there are so many so closely grouped at Machrie Moor.

One other mysterious monument dating probably to the earlier Bronze Age, remains to be considered. In a plantation at Stronach up behind Brodick School *(003364)*, there is to be seen a strangely assorted collection of designs on a large scale, pecked out on a wide, gently sloping, rock surface. The "carvings" were illustrated in *The Book of Arran* and comprise forms not unlike a huge key-hole, double penannular rings and small cups. Examples of comparable decorated surfaces occur notably at Kilmichael Glassary and other sites in Mid-Argyll, and again around Gatehouse of Fleet. Boulders with man-made cup markings on them are common in various parts of Scotland, including Kintyre, but they seem to be scarce in Arran.

In review it may be remarked that while the Bronze Age has left behind many tantalising questions for which no solution may be in sight, archaeologists have found the period extraordinarily interesting. This is partly due to the number of the monuments as here in Arran, but also because so many objects of bronze and gold have preserved their form in a recognisable shape after three and even four thousand years. They have corroded far more slowly than iron so that even the casting methods can be worked out, while studies of typology are greatly facilitated. Perhaps it may be added that in looking at the bronzes in a museum which usually have a dull brown colour (with patches of bright green if they need conservation), the metal of a sword or axe head when new and polished, could be made to gleam like gold itself.

4
A PILGRIMAGE TO MACHRIE MOOR

Machrie Moor is astonishing from an archaeological point of view. The number and variety of the monuments which are strung out over an area of not much more than a mile, are most extraordinary. No one monument in itself could really be described as spectacular, and none has been set out by the Department of the Environment, but the group as a whole deserves more publicity than it has so far received. Access is by means of a farm road and a track which are signposted some three miles (5 km.) north of Blackwaterfoot on the Machrie road, as leading to the stone circles. There is a right of way, but cars are not allowed, and visitors should be careful to close all gates. A walk of about two hours is involved for a quick survey, partly over a track and partly over peat-moor *(Fig. 4.1)*.

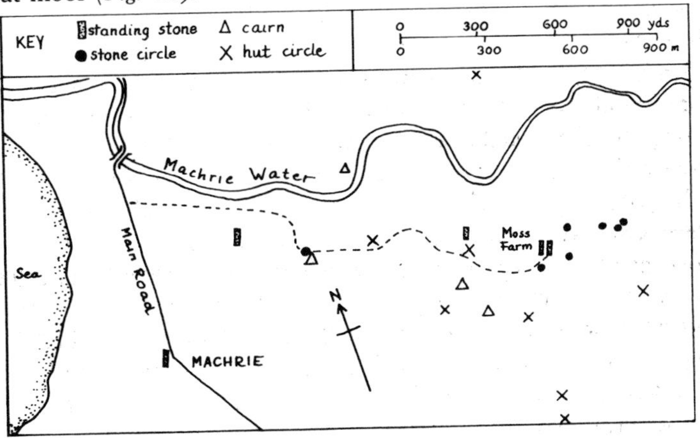

Fig. 4.1 **Excursion route to Machrie Moor**

The side road first crosses arable land, with the remnants of a cairn just recognisable across the Machrie Water. The ground rapidly deteriorates to rough pasture, and then gives place to the open moor. this point *(901327)* a circle of boulders is actually crossed by the track; it surrounds a denuded cairn which, at the time of writing, was being excavated under the direction of Dr. Burl, an authority on stone circles. The moor itself is undulating ground with a thick layer of peat in the hollows especially. It has been a source of fuel in the past and the air photograph of the area shows that there is a maze of old peat cuttings which seem to dominate the landscape. In ancient times the hollows must have been marshy, and it is necessary to visualise the monuments as occurring on the higher, drier areas. Studies of the peat and of the pollen preserved in it, are in progress, and should eventually give an idea of the history of the vegetation and also of man's activity in modifying the natural environment. Various sites of hut-circles can be picked out on an air photograph of this moorland, but for the most part they are very difficult to locate on the ground.

Several examples of hut-circles can, however, be reached easily from the track. One which, unfortunately, is not very obvious, lies just north of the track where it begins to rise to a low hill *(at about 903326)*. The site takes the form of a rough circular platform, the upper end of which has been cut into a slope to provide a horizontal surface. Two more hut-circles occur just north of the track as it reaches the gate through the fence enclosing the grazing land around the old and now derelict Moss Farm. Both are easily missed unless attention is drawn to this patch of ground, but the one nearest the track and only about 10 metres away is quite obvious. It is about 10 m. across and is enclosed by a low bank with a gap for the doorway in the south eastern side. A few metres to the north is a very ragged example, and then, nearby, is an isolated standing stone, probably of Bronze Age date. Also, there is a very recent commemorative slab erected to the memory of the late John Boscawen, where there is a wide prospect over the moorland and the old farm fields.

Looking southwards from the gate through the fence, there is an electric fence running west–east about 50 m. away, and on the far side are the much denuded remains of a long cairn, the first of the Neolithic monuments, though the chamber has been destroyed almost completely.

It is known as the Moss Farm Cairn. Proceeding through the gate for about 200 m., there appears on the southern edge of the track by a scrubby hawthorn, the remnants of a large chamber with one huge slab. Looking across the track, at the grass rather than at any noticeable mound, it is possible to detect the remnants of what appears to be a cairn. In the writer's opinion, at least, the site is that of another Neolithic chambered cairn. Away to the south about 300 m. distant, and on the wrong side of the electric fence, a green mound rises out of the moor. In the centre there is a single elongated chamber of yet another Neolithic tomb referred to as Tormore No.2. In its simplicity, it may be taken to represent an early stage in tomb development here in Arran.

The first of the main series of stone circles is reached where the track bends sharply towards the deserted farm buildings *(908324)*. A remarkable monument it is, though it consists of rough boulders. There are two concentric rings, the inner one strictly circular while the outer is slightly egg-shaped in plan on very careful measurement *(Fig 3.16)*. One of the stones on the south side has a curious cylindrical hole near the edge; traditionally, this is where Fingal, a Celtic hero of Iron Age times, tied up his dog, and the circle generally is known as Fingal's Cauldron Seat. Looking eastwards across the moor, with a magnificent panorama of hills in the background, the sites of five other stone circles can be seen, all within a distance of some 300 m. The whole setting is most memorable, and it can only be hoped that an open view will be preserved for future generations. In the distance, away to the north, is the circle at Auchagallan, while a mile (1600 m.) to the south is the Neolithic chambered tomb of Tormore No.1. To the west rises the hill known as Tormore, with its hut-circles and field systems.

From the double ring of boulders, keeping straight on to the east as the track bends off to the north, the route crosses an old field boundary and then there is the remnant of another, rather small circle of boulders. When excavation took place over a hundred years ago, a cinerary urn was found, and a bronze pin, suggesting that it might be a little later than the others, or perhaps the interment was later. Looking now to the north east, there rises out of the moor a single huge slab of sandstone, much weathered. Investigations have shown that there were once nine stones and two cists were found within. Dr. Roy's careful survey recently has shown that the pattern is egg-shaped, precisely as with the outer ring of the double circle, though the sizes differ. This part of the moor is badly cut up by old peat workings, which are apt to be very wet. A third circle, just a short distance away, is the most impressive of all, though only three stones are now upstanding *(Fig. 4.2),* but they are very large slabs of which one is weathered into strange grooves. A cist containing a Food Vessel was found at the centre. Lying at the circle is a large round slab, cracked across a central perforation. This is definitely not, as speculation has suggested, an altar used by druids when cutting the throat of a luckless maiden, but an uncompleted mill-stone, presumably made from one of the uprights and abandoned after breakage.

The fifth "circle" at the eastern end of the series *(913324),* greatly intrigued Dr. Roy. He found that it was, in fact, a perfect ellipse which, he pointed out, could be made by using two stakes and a length of cord in a great loop of the appropriate size which, when stretched taut, could be used to mark out the pattern. In addition, the rough stones of the "circle", which are not particularly large, are arranged in a way which is unique on the moor, a sandstone slab alternating with a granite boulder. At present, the site is being re-excavated by Dr. Burl and no cist has been found. While investigating what was thought to be an outlaying slab nearby, it was found to belong to yet another circle to add to the five described in *The Book of Arran.* Dr. Burl's party discovered that there may, in fact, be yet another in rather wet ground to the north of the main group. . Who can tell what the blanket of peat may hide in this extraordinary moorland?

At this point, the majority of visitors re-trace their steps to the main road as the continuation of the route eastwards to the String road across the moor would be a penance rather than a pilgrimage. However, somewhere in the moor there appears to be yet another site of which two stones only remain,as reported in *The Book of Arran;* but where? Really, the proliferation of circles in this small area of Arran verges on the unbelievable!

Fig. 4.2 **Standing stones, Machrie Moor**

5
THE IRON AGE – FORTS AND DUNS

In the later stages of the Bronze Age, the character of the archaeological record begins to change. Not a great deal is to be learned now about the mode of life from the cremation burials of the period, and in Scotland generally, few habitation sites have been excavated with modern technique. On the other hand, the metal workers in bronze of both weapons and ornaments were obviously highly skilled in their craft, and many objects have been recovered and placed in our museums.

It used to be accepted that the succeeding Iron Age was ushered in about 500 B.C. by Celtic speaking invaders, first of all reaching southern and then western England. Later, chieftains and their war bands were thought to have penetrated northwards, some reaching North Britain from the south while others worked along theAtlantic seaboard, ultimately reaching as far as Shetland. These Celtic invaders would seem to have brought new art forms and to have been responsible for the introduction of innumerable fortified enclosures which are known in Scotland as forts, duns or brochs, according to variety. Certainly a period of social insecurity necessitating these enclosures followed in the Iron Age, and we know from literary sources that Celtic chieftains, here and on the Continent, fought for the glory of it and were notorious for their cattle raiding. Society was one of sharp class distinctions with the champions, the knightly warriors and the druids (priests and teachers) at the top; below came the freemen and farmers, and then the serfs and slaves.

During the last decade or so, much of what had been taken for granted by archaeologists and seemed to be supported by the writings of classical authors, has been questioned very seriously. Fortification has been found by Carbon Fourteen datings to have commenced in the late Bronze Age. The old idea that great social change must have been the result of invasions like those of the Anglo-Saxons as told by Bede, is now rather discredited. Contacts by trade through small-scale movements and changes brought about by copying the techniques of others, as well as local invention, are now being considered far more seriously. In Scotland especially, the total amount of evidence for mass invasions is very small, while continuity from the past is important. It is even questionable whether the introduction of a Celtic language can be safely placed as in the Iron Age; Scottish Gaelic resembles that of Ireland whence it appears to have spread in later times.

This long introduction on recent developments has been necessary to explain the difference in attitude of archaeologists since Gordon Childe, the author of *The Prehistory of Scotland* in 1935, first brought Scottish prehistoric archaeology into line with that of Western Europe generally. Much that this great teacher wrote is memorable still, but particularly when dealing with places such as Arran where research and excavation into the local Iron Age have scarcely begun, it is necessary to avoid applying to the island generalisations which are now outdated, stemming from the days of "*Prehistory*". It may seem frustrating to the amateur that clear-cut accounts of what actually happened cannot yet be given, but much field work and research is necessary to clarify a very complex situation. What is obvious is that the increasing use of iron after about 500 B.C. was only one aspect of great changes in the archaeological record generally. To speak of this period as "Celtic Britain" as some writers have done, begs the question of when the Celtic speakers arrived. Let us turn first to the use of iron itself.

In ancient times, iron proved difficult to make into tools, for unlike tin or copper, only a cindery mass resulted from first smelting the ore. The Hittites of Biblical times were amongst the first to make effective use of iron by reheating the material from the furnace, hammering out the impurities and gradually welding the remaining metal into a useful tool. The ore is common and once the smith's technique was learned, metal became much less expensive. But iron could not be cast into a durable tool, it had to be forged, that is, hammered to shape so that new forms had to be evolved. Socketed axes such as were in use in the later

Bronze Age, were difficult to shape in iron and a flat form hafted like a modern axe, had to be used. Itinerant smiths probably played a large part in spreading the use of iron. Unfortunately from the archaeological point of view, iron soon rusts away under normal conditions, and on many Iron Age sites in Scotland, very little has survived. Bronze, however, continued in use for ornaments, employing new art forms from those of the late Bronze Age, and these have proved useful in recognising a typology for the Iron Age. Pottery, especially in southern Scotland, is often very poorly fired and far behind the wares of the Neolithic and Early Bronze Age in quality. Moreover it has little in the way of decoration here in the south to help in placing it in a sequence. Dating Iron Age sites has proved extremely difficult and even now it is to be emphasised that Carbon Fourteen gives only a broad range in the time scale.

A poor prospect indeed appears to open up for a section here on the local Iron Age, but in spite of the almost complete absence to date of modern excavation and of museum pieces, the field monuments are both substantial and surprisingly variable. The sites recognisable as of Iron Age date consist almost entirely of fortified enclosures, and so far there appears to be a complete absence of certain other well known types of monument, for instance, the souterrains or earth houses, the crannogs or lake dwellings and the wheelhouses of the north. Some of the island hut-circles may belong to the period but the limited excavations up to date have not as yet placed any one example in the Iron Age. However, the contrasts between the individual enclosures on the island are so considerable and capable of being traced on the ground by the amateur, that it seems worth while to take most of them in turn, especially as they usually occupy extraordinarily good viewpoints. But first of all some comment is required as to how and why they were built.

It is necessary to get away from the idea that these so-called "forts" were all built at the one time to protect Arran's shores from mass invasion. Almost certainly they were built individually over a very long series of years. Their main purpose was to act as strongholds, the smallest being no more than fortified homesteads, while the largest could hold a considerable community and livestock as well. There is no evidence to suggest that they would withstand a siege, and often there was no water supply. With cattle and slave raiding the order of the day, if a sudden onslaught did not succeed, the attackers themselves would quickly find themselves without food.

In Britain, generally, these fortified enclosures take many forms. There may have been a steep-sided ditch, the earth from which had been piled up to make a bank, usually on the inside, creating a further obstacle to assailants from without. Often such a ditch and earthen bank have been duplicated, or even repeated several times. Weathering, over the centuries, may almost have obliterated the site on the ground, but it can often be detected on air photographs as the different depth of soil on ditch and bank tends to be reflected in the vegetation, perhaps as a "crop mark" in a cornfield. Normally in the west of Scotland, reliance for defence was placed on a thick stone wall perhaps with a ditch utilising natural hollows wherever possible in the hard ground. The wall was built without mortar, and was constructed with large, carefully laid slabs or blocks of stone to form the inner and outer face, whereas the interior was filled with earth, rubble, boulders and, in fact, anything available. In the long ages since these walls were built, the rain, frost and wind have caused the retaining stones in the facings to slip and give way, so that the core has often spilled outwards. So often on Iron Age sites a wall, formerly more than 2 m. high, appears to be no more than a bank of stones and earth, largely overgrown. Such walls again may be duplicated, and indeed the White Caterthun near Brechin has five rings of defences, of which the inmost is reckoned to be the most imposing in Britain. Somewhere along the wall or bank there would be an entrance or entrances, formerly closed by a wooden gate; now the feature is marked only by a gap if it appears at all. To add to the problem of interpretation, many of the walls and ditches have been purposely levelled over the centuries, being robbed for building stone for houses, field dykes and roads.

In field studies, there is a great fascination in trying to visualise a fortified site as it would be in its hey-day, and to imagine the Iron Age commander standing on the top of his wall, spitting defiance at the enemy while his men used sling stones, arrows and spears to hurl at their foes. They, in their turn, would throw everything they had at the defenders, and then try to rush a weak section of the walling. All this in theory, but in practice numbers of these forts seem to have been sited in very odd places, overlooked from behind or tactically weak in some rather obvious places. It is difficult to avoid the conclusion that it was the *appearance of strength* that mattered, to deter an enemy attack by an awesome look, just as the Medieval castles of later centuries were calculated to achieve. In examining the defences of individual forts, especially amongst a group as varied as we have in Arran, it is possible to appreciate something of the spirit of the times, to sense a little of the hopes and fears of the defenders. It is far more difficult to try to fathom the ritual significance and the religious ideas of the builders of the chambered tombs and stone circles.

Within the limits of the fortified enclosures, little is to be seen on a great many of these sites to suggest where the occupants found shelter, whether temporary or permanent quarters. Sometimes, as on the very large fort on the northern peak of the Eildons in the Borders, many floors of buildings have been detected, in this case as many as three hundred. In the majority of cases, however, the relatively flimsy walls of these interior structures have left no obvious trace. The very small forts or "duns" which are little larger than a hut-circle, could easily have been roofed over completely. Excavation is normally needed to find the foundations, floors and post-holes for supports for the roof, and as any one site may have been re-occupied perhaps over a period of centuries, the task of disentangling the evidence can be very difficult. Nothing of this complexity has been noted in the one or two forts which have been superficially investigated in Arran, but one which was excavated under the direction of the author at Kildonan Bay in Kintyre, opposite Blackwaterfoot, illustrates the point. It was first constructed in the Iron Age, and was then reconditioned in about the 7th century A.D. at the time of the Scots of Dalriada; it was re-occupied as a homestead again in the 14th century. Another little dun at Ugadale, on the same bay, was occupied after long intervals, as late as the 16th century.

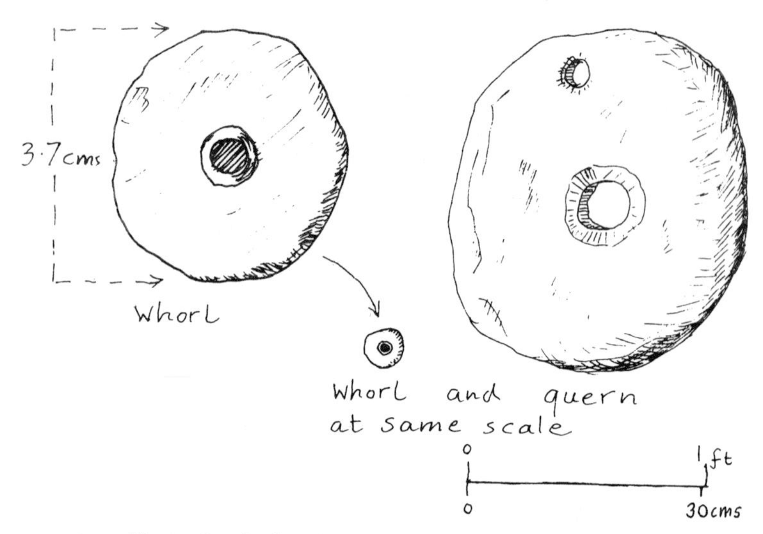

Fig. 5.1 **A spindle whorl and upper stone of a quern**

Although we have no direct evidence from Arran, considerable numbers of Iron Age forts, duns, brochs, crannogs or lake dwellings and souterrains or earth houses, have been excavated in Scotland, and have provided a mass of material, much of which is preserved in the National Museum of Antiquities in Edinburgh. Regional differences can be found amongst the various types of pottery and domestic refuse which have been recovered in these investigations, but in general, the basic culture, the Iron Age way of life, has been found to be fundamentally the same throughout. We can say with conviction that the fort builders in Arran would possess domestic animals, including cattle, sheep, goats, horses and pigs, and would produce cereal crops, especially barley. The grain would be prepared in the earlier days by rubbing it down on a slightly hollowed stone known as a saddle quern, but later in the Iron Age the circular quern was introduced and finds of these have often occurred *(Fig 5.1)*. Pottery was very common on northern sites but may be quite scarce in southern Scotland, and may

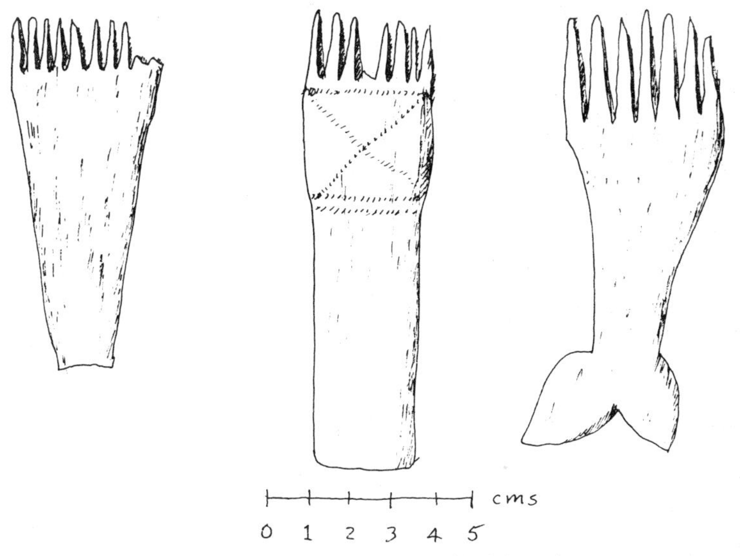

Fig. 5.2 **Weaving combs of antler (Caithness)**

be very poor on these sites. Iron was smelted and forged locally, and traces of slag and furnace residue are frequently noted. Wool was spun and woven, the little circular stone whorls *(Fig 5.1)* used to weight the spindle on which the yarn was wound by hand, are common finds. Stone continued in use for many everyday objects, and bone was the normal material for pins, needles, weaving combs and borers *(Fig. 5.2)*. Wood and leather were almost certainly used in quantity, but in the majority of cases have perished without trace.

It is, of course, difficult to visualise life actually going on within these Iron Age fortifications, so many of which have survived in bleak places, and the walls have been reduced to a tumble of stones. Nevertheless, these people were not savages living a hand-to-mouth existence. Their ornaments, and particularly their horse trappings, could be artistic achievements in bronze. They certainly possessed a tribal organisation and, indeed, some of the largest and most advanced of the hill forts, at least in southern Britain, were approaching closely to a form of town life.

Turning now to our local sites *(Fig. 5.3)* the largest fort by far in Arran is that on the headland at Drumadoon *(886293)*, reached either by the shore or the golf course from Blackwaterfoot. The seaward side needed no artificial protection, as the columnar basalt cliff, which is such a spectacular feature, was more than sufficient. The ruin of a single wall can be traced round the long landward side, forming a great loop enclosing a space of about twelve acres. On ascending the headland from the neighbourhood of the far green on the golf course, passing a small quarry, now abandoned, a low line of slabs marks the site of what would once be a wall, anything between two and four metres thick. Further along, to the north, the walling appears as a much overgrown bank with a level grassy terrace on the upper side. A break in the bank wide enough to let a cart through probably represents the ancient gateway. Much of the enclosure is very rocky ground indeed, and although it is possible to imagine small houses nestling in some of the hollows, there is no sign of foundations, and perhaps the dwellings were built along the inner side of the wall. Drumadoon (hill of the fort) is so large that it may have been something in the nature of a tribal centre. Perhaps the island's overlord lived here where his numerous cattle could be herded within the fort. The great length of wall was intended both for protection of the local people in times of danger, and to demonstrate the lord's power and wealth. There is a magnificent outlook over the lands around Blackwaterfoot, over to Kintyre, and away to Antrim on a clear day. Probably the dependants cultivated the ground now forming the green fields of Drumadoon Farm, but to the north, in what is now moorland, there are a number of hut-circles, some of which could conceivably date to this period. Perhaps one day this wonderful untouched site will attract its excavators, but seasons of work are involved.

Drumadoon is very much exposed to the wild storms of winter, but even more remarkable from this point of view is a site 3.5 km. directly inland, at a height of over 200 m. *(920292)*. It is on a hill top

THE IRON AGE – FORTS AND DUNS

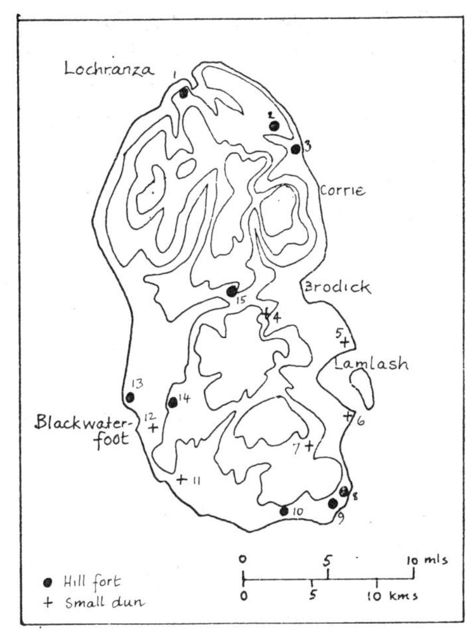

		Nat. Grid	
1.	**Lochranza**	*927503*	Hill top, rampart on one side only
2.	**North Glen Sannox**	*002474*	Hill top, annexe at either end
3.	**An Cnap, Sannox**	*017461*	Cliff top, vitrified rampart, hard to recognise
4.	**Glen Cloy 'Bruce's castle'**	*992339*	Slight traces on natural mound
5.	**Dun Fionn**	*047339*	Very small enclosure on cliff top
6.	**King's Cross Point**	*056283*	Remains of small circular fort on sloping rock
7.	**Glenashdale**	*031252*	Rampart crossing the neck of a promontory in the plantation
8.	**Dippin**	*051224*	Cliff top enclosure badly overgrown
9.	**Kildonan**	*044219*	Cliff top enclosure
10.	**Bennan Head**	*998208*	Cliff top, traces of several ramparts
11.	**Torr a Chaisteil, Corriecravie**	*922233*	Remains of small circular dun on top of natural hillock
12.	**Kilpatrick**	*905266*	Small enclosure possibly occupied in the Iron Age
13.	**Drumadoon**	*886293*	Single rampart on cliff top, possibly a tribal capital
14.	**Cnoc Ballygown**	*920292*	Hill top enclosure probably an unfinished fort
15.	**Cnoc a' Chlochair, Monyquil**	*953358*	Enclosure on mound divided by cross wall

Fig. 5.3 **Distribution of Iron Age forts**

overlooking the Shiskine valley above the farm of Ballygown: the enclosure is large and of exceptional interest. Running round the top of the hill, the outline has been marked out simply by a series of ditches in alignment, the individual ditch lengths being separated by short, uncut sections, like bridges. The upcast has been thrown out to form low banks along the edges of the ditches. The current explanation is that we have here a rare example of a fort which had only just been started when further progress was stopped. Perhaps the wet and wind of an Arran winter, and the distance from arable land overcame the obsession with the appearance of strength on this high hill site, and it is tempting to think that Drumadoon emerged as a better proposition.

Another fort on an exposed hill top occurs high above Lochranza on the south side of the bay, at an altitude approaching 200 m. *(927503)*. It is a long, narrow enclosure on rocky ground, formed by a badly ruined wall on one side where it is almost concealed in the bracken, and by the very steep natural slope on the other. The view over the bay and the castle gives fresh perspective in appreciating the later Medieval site. For some reason, the old fort has been omitted from the later O.S. maps, though it is described in *The Book of Arran.*

Very different in plan, as shown in *The Book of Arran,* is the next fort on our itinerary, which occupies an irregular rocky eminence overlooking North Glen Sannox *(002474) (Fig. 5.4)*. It can be approached by slanting north eastwards up the hill from the road bridge half way up the glen, but it is found more easily by keeping along the north side of the river until the site of the Clearance village is reached, and then by striking boldly uphill, easing the slope by taking a zig-zag course slowly; the view over the Arran peaks is worth every upward step. The eminence in question is not the highest in the neighbourhood, and the fort is somewhat overlooked from the west, but from well outside any missile range of those days. The enclosure is smaller than those considered so far, and is elongated, utilising very effectively the natural rock faces and steep slopes. There is a central oval space, and at either end an annexe, extending the oval shape. The entrance has been at the eastern end. The curious little structure built into the ruined wall on the west of the central area is relatively modern. What purpose

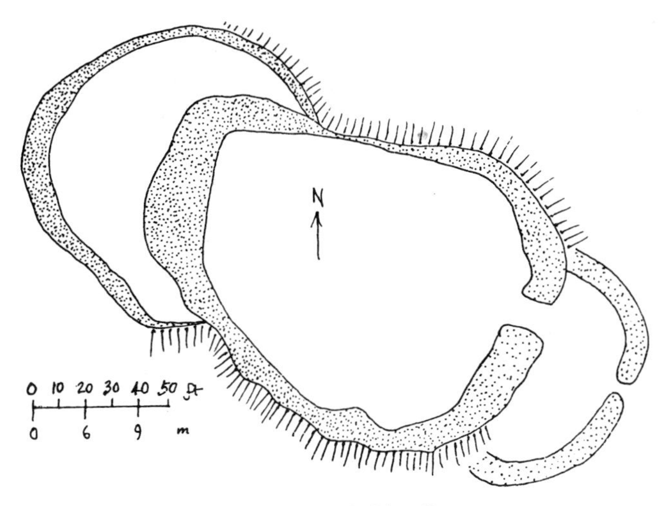

Fig. 5.4 **Hill Fort at North Glen Sannox**

this fort could have served on its high moorland site is difficult to imagine; perhaps it might have been used to protect the cattle grazing on the high pasture during the summer, the counterpart of the later shielings.

Two other inland sites, somewhat comparable in size, may be briefly noted at this stage. One is located to the east of the farm of Monyquil on a hillock *(953358)*. It has a view down the Machrie Water, but is overlooked from the high ground to the north of the String road as it climbs to the summit on the way to Brodick. There is a very ruinous wall, much hidden by bracken, with the main enclosure sub-divided by a partition. The second fort is located in Glenashdale on an eminence facing southwards across the burn just below the falls *(031252)*. The site can be viewed from the Forestry road, but it is at present planted with trees. The defences consist of a single thick wall crossing the neck of the promontory occupied by the fort, the ground falling steeply away and needing no further fortification. A superficial excavation was carried out many years ago, but little was found except evidence of use as an iron smelting site, probably in much later times.

Very different from those discussed so far is the fort on the headland north of Sannox Bay *(017461)*. It can be reached by a rough track leaving the main road just north of the small Sannox Church, on the upper side of a stone dyke. The site passed unnoticed until the twenties, when pieces of slag-like material mixed with burnt stone were recognised as evidence of vitrification. Excavation then confirmed that the headland was, in fact, enclosed by a defensive system, the cliff forming the seaward side, measuring about 30 m. overall. What is to be seen now of the man-made defences consists of two low mounds about 3 m. apart, sometimes with a boulder, or in one place, a row of boulders, showing in the bracken under the trees. With difficulty, these can be traced from cliff to cliff, but are very low. Vitrification can be seen on the western limit of the enclosure, but the excavators found masses in between the two mounds. Nowadays, vitrification is recognised, not as a purposeful method of strengthening the rampart, but as the result of a conflagration, probably accidental, of a stone wall which has been tied together by cross timbers. The unusual feature at Sannox is the slight appearance of the defences now, and it might be suggested that the original rampart would have been built with an unusual amount of timber to strengthen it, and perhaps with plentiful use of turf in the filling.

These vitrified forts in Scotland belong to a group now described as timber-laced. Probably vitrification occurred in a high wind when the temperature would reach sufficiently high to fuse stone. A group of these forts exists around the Firth of Clyde; there is one on Carradale Island, one near Hunterston, while the most famous, Dunagoil, lies on a rocky ridge directly opposite the Sannox fort at the south end of the island of Bute. It was excavated years ago and the numerous finds are in Rothesay Museum. Recent work suggests that at least some of these timber-laced forts were built at a relatively early date, Carbon Fourteen results indicating construction in the 7th century B.C.

At the opposite extreme in fort building is the minute enclosure of Dun Fionn at the summit of the path over the headland between Brodick and Lamlash via Corrygills *(047339)*. It is a remarkable

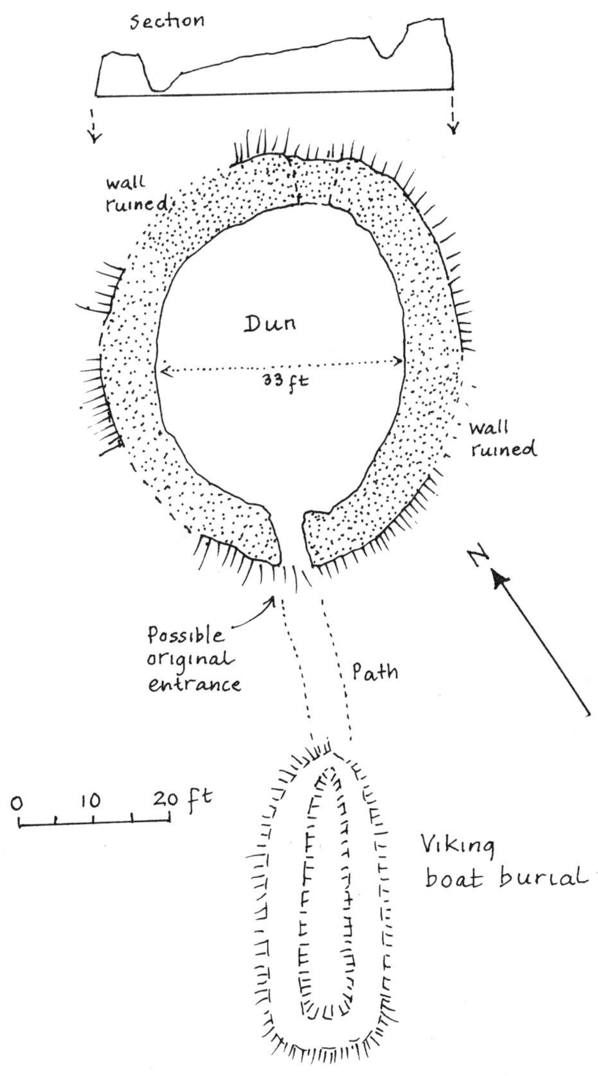

Fig. 5.5 **Dun and Viking Burial at Kings Cross Point (Fairhurst & Forbes)**

position on the very edge of the high cliff facing the sea. All that exists is a low bank enclosing a hollow oval space no bigger than the interior of a hut-circle. Apart from the bank, the defences consist of the natural steep slopes of the pronounced hillock on which the dùn stands. The tremendous view over both Brodick Bay and the Holy Island as well as towards the Ayrshire coast, suggests the need for a look-out post.

Almost at the tip of the rocky point at King's Cross, on the opposite side of Lamlash Bay, is yet another type of fort which unfortunately is in a very ruinous condition. It almost adjoins the site of the Viking boat burial to be described later *(056283) (Fig. 5.5)*. This little dun is only about 11 m. across internally, again, much the size of a hut-circle, and it is more or less circular in spite of the fact that it occupies the summit of an elongated ridge. The enclosure is on a steeply sloping rock face, and when excavated years ago very little was found, possibly because the excavators were digging up a filling made to provide a level interior. The wall on the down side of the slope stands up well in the undergrowth and is nearly 4 m. thick, but the upper or south side is ruined down to the foundations. A path goes through both it and the Viking site to the west, but very few visitors recognise the existence of the monuments and they are now so dilapidated that little can be done by way of conservation.

Another small dun near Corriecravie calls for comment at this point as it, again, is circular *(922233)*. It overlooks the low ground representing raised beach material, from a steep sided hillock which has been detached from the adjacent ground by erosion. This hillock is visible from the main road from Kildonan just before Corriecravie is reached, and is signposted as "Torr a' Chaisteil"; it is under the protection of the Department of the Environment. The steep sided hillock has a profusion of little ledges in the turf; they have nothing to do with the Iron Age. The natural defences would seem to have been very strong in themselves, but on the square top of the hillock there are the remains of a circular dun with a wall over 3 m. thick; a high bank just outside seems to suggest an outwork, but it may be natural. This site reminds the writer very strongly of the dun on Kildonan Bay, Kintyre, which had a cell, a double stairway and a narrow gallery in the thickness of the wall. In fact, the remains are not unlike those of a broch, for although these high circular structures are most common in the far north of Scotland, examples do occur in the south, for instance at Dunburgidale in Bute. In some ways, this Corriecravie dun is the most intriguing fort on the island of Arran.

Two sites on the edge of the cliffs between Whiting Bay and Kildonan may be referred to briefly. Both are rather small promontory forts and neither is accessible to the public. One lies immediately north of Dippin Lodge *(051224)* but it is in a thicket which makes observation difficult, though the site appears to be very strongly defended naturally. The other lies nearer the road down to Kildonan *(044219)*. Finally, there is a fort on the edge of the cliff up on Bennan Head, the site of which is conspicuous from a distance as it rises above the general level of the skyline as a small, steep-sided crag which tends to attract the eye *(998208)*. It is noteworthy amongst the island sites as being the only one to have multiple defensive walls. They appear as low, smooth banks looping around the crag, and have suffered badly in the past. Usually sites with multiple defences around them involve a much larger area, and it has been suggested that part of the crag has collapsed down the cliff. No sign of such a collapse, and no obvious scar can be noted, and the site certainly provides a problem.

In reviewing the situation as a whole, two stretches of ground which would appear in general terms to have been favourable to the settlement of Iron Age peoples, are not adequately represented in sites of fortified enclosures. One is the area around Brodick where only one small fort is known away up Glen Cloy *(992339)*; it is now so ruinous that the position on a hillock can be located only with difficulty. The other area lies between the fort at Drumadoon and the one at Lochranza, where not one single site has so far been recognised. The terrain resembles that on the coasts of Kintyre where little duns and occasional larger forts occur at short intervals.

As regards accessible sites, all have been discussed briefly in the foregoing account. Perhaps the following might be especially recommended, partly because of their intrinsic interest, and partly because a visit will be rewarded with an unusually attractive viewpoint:—

Drumadoon, Lochranza, North Glen Sannox, Sannox vitrified fort, Dun Fionn, King's Cross and Corriecravie. With our brief notes, it is hoped that the interested visitor will be able to find those sites which the Ordnance Survey map indicates clearly enough, but groups them under the somewhat cryptic "fort" and "dun". The variety of these enclosures both as regards size and form is such that the bemused amateur finds it hard to accept them as a group, all attributable to a society flourishing two thousand years ago. The variety of the Arran sites is astonishing, but as yet ideas on typology scarcely allow more than a guess at the relative age. Some vitrified forts may be very early but not all: broch-like structures such as Corriecravie seem to belong to the end of the Pre-Christian era, or even later: single walled forts such as Drumadoon may be earlier: all may have a complicated history of re-occupation over centuries. A survey of the Arran sites certainly brings home very clearly the amount of investigation which faces the archaeologist of the Iron Age in Northern Britain.

6
ROMANS, EARLY CHRISTIANS AND VIKINGS

In 79 or 80 A.D., the Roman governor of Britain, Agricola, is recorded by his son-in-law, Tacitus, as moving his forces into Scotland. Four years later a battle was fought somewhere north of the Tay, which, for the time being, marked the end of native resistance. During the next half century the Romans lost their grip on territories north of the line chosen in the time of Hadrian as marking the limit of the Empire. A re-advance took place in 139 A.D., to a line from the Forth to the Clyde which was fortified by a wall and closely set forts — the Antonine frontier. This seems to have been held for about forty years, and then the Romans retired once more to the Hadrianic frontier from the Solway to the Tyne.

The Roman occupation directly affected what we now know as southern Scotland for little more than one hundred years all told, but archaeologically the period is a landmark. The occurrence of scraps of bright red Samian ware has been noted on Iron Age sites from Kintyre to the Northern Isles and provides a very important dating horizon as between an earlier and a later Iron Age. Roman mass manufactures obviously penetrated well beyond Hadrian's or even the Antonine wall, but beyond the latter the native tribes continued to live much as before, so that without the Roman horizon, it is difficult to distinguish native archaeological material as being before, during or after the conquest.

The Island of Arran appears never to have been included within the Empire, but it is reasonable to suppose that the fleet would patrol the Firth of Clyde, and a harbour is suspected directly across at Irvine. Equally reasonable seems the suggestion that Lamlash Bay, one of the finest natural harbours along the whole west coast of Europe, would at times be utilised for shelter by the fleet as an occasional refuge in adverse weather. Nothing has turned up on the island to attest a

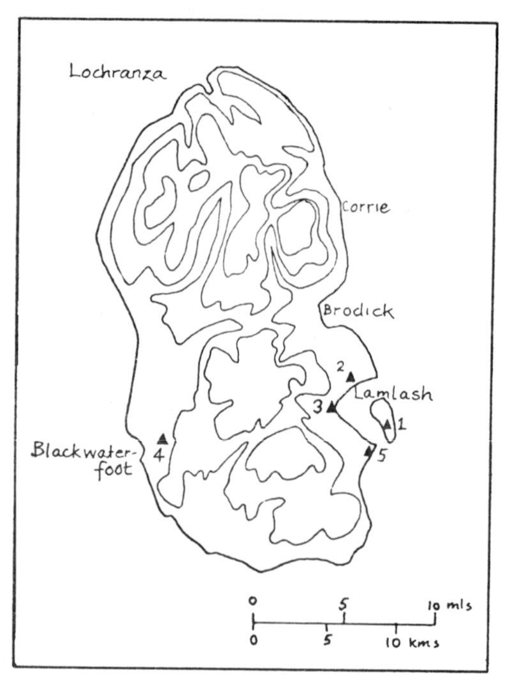

		Nat. Grid	
1.	**Holy Isle**	*060295*	Cave of St. Molaise and Norse runes
2.	**Lamlash, Blairmore**	*032323*	Old St. Bride's Church
3.	**Lamlash, Kilbride Parish Church**	*026309*	Carved stone cross in churchyard
4.	**Shiskine, St. Molio's Church**	*910295*	Carving of a prior built into wall
5.	**King's Cross Point**	*056283*	Viking Boat-burial

Fig. 6.1 **Distribution of early Christian and Viking sites**

Roman presence, but trade, pillage and slave raiding very probably occurred from and on Arran. Any trace of temporary occupation at Lamlash would, of course, be found only by a remote chance.

Scholars have now no doubt that Christianity reached the northern frontier of the Roman province well before the end of the occupation of Britain. St. Ninian's name has been associated with Whithorn and St.

Patrick seems to have been abducted to Ireland from the Clyde area. Only later did influences from Iona reach southwards to Arran, and our earliest known disciple, the legendary St. Molaise or Molio, may have lived amongst a people already converted to the faith. In any case his sojourn in the island would be that of a hermit seeking seclusion for meditation rather than as an evangelist. When he came and who he was is by no means certain, but before discussing him further, a brief look is necessary at the times in which he lived. *(Fig. 6.1* shows the distribution of Christian and Viking sites).

In the 6th century, Scots coming from northern Ireland had taken over control of what is now Argyll to form their kingdom of Dalriada. They and the subject population came, in the course of time, to speak Gaelic, a Celtic language very closely related to that spoken in Ireland. On the mainland, the Britons of the kingdom of Strathclyde spoke a language more closely allied to Welsh. Arran, in later times, was occupied by Gaelic speakers, the Celtic place names are Gaelic, and apparently we must associate the island in Early Christian times with the kingdom of the Scots and with the form of Christianity followed by St. Columba and the monastery of Iona. Of the Scots themselves, little has been discovered by the archaeologist. Their capital at Dunadd on Loch Crinan has been excavated, but only a few other sites have been investigated; one of them is that little dun with broch-like features in Kintyre, opposite Machrie. Here a re-organisation of the Iron Age enclosure took place in the 6th or 7th century A.D., and it is tempting to think that it was given to hermits who occupied it as a 'kil' — hence the name Kildonan, the cell of St. Donan.

The only St. Molaise of note mentioned in the monastic records, died as abbot of a monastery in western Ireland. He may, as a young priest, have sought solitude as far away as Arran, that is not impossible. The place name Lamlash, a corruption of 'Eilan nam Molaise' and the *Holy* Island, can hardly be dismissed as an invention of folk lore. Then there is his cave to which innumerable visitors have crossed from Lamlash to the Holy Island. It is, in fact, little more than a rock shelter eroded into the sandstone, and it is a most undesirable residence by modern standards. But the saints and hermits of those days were made of very stern stuff indeed, and local legend is reinforced by a number of ancient crosses cut into the layer of rock forming the roof of the cave, by pilgrims in later times. Amongst numerous initials cut by recent vandals, there is vaguely traceable some Norse lettering (to be discussed later) which seems to indicate that in the 13th century the cave had special significance. It has been excavated on two separate occasions, but little evidence of value was recovered other than to emphasise the stark austerity of the hermit's dwelling.

There is also an obscure reference in 1594 to a 'friary' on the Holy Island. Friars had their centres in towns, since they begged for a living, not on remote spots like the Holy Island. Recent archaeological research on the period would suggest a possible sequence. The Early Christians were obsessed by the notion of the sanctity of relics and the very fact of burial in ground with sanctity through proximity to a hermit's cave, may have led to the establishment of a cemetery. Later a chapel for the benefit of pilgrims may have been built and have continued in some form to the time of the Reformation. It is relevant to note that people were buried on the Holy Island long afterwards until a funeral party was drowned in the crossing.

Many years ago, a number of slab-lined graves were found near Kildonan farmhouse, and excavation revealed an apse-like structure which was thought to be the remains of a chapel. The graves are of a type known as long cists which are often grouped together, with an orientation towards the east. They are unlike the cists of the Bronze Age and seem to belong to the Early Christian period. Again there may be evidence of a kil, presumably dedicated to St. Donan. Perhaps one day soon, further excavation with modern techniques may be attempted here, and especially on the Holy Island.

Another site which must be noted at this stage is the King's Cave on the shore between Blackwaterfoot and Machrie. A path well frequented in the summer leads past it; the approach from the south is via the top of Drumadoon headland and thence along the raised shore line. The cave is, by local legend, one of the numerous places where Bruce was inspired by the persistence of the spider, but our story begins much

Fig. 6.2 **Symbols in King's Cave, Machrie. Ogham Script**

earlier. Most visitors end the pilgrimage to the scene of Bruce's refuge by leaving the cave as quickly as possible because of the musty smell. The archaeologist will be rewarded by a stay of twenty minutes to allow the eyes to become accustomed to the dim light. There are, in fact, two adjacent caves, of which the northerly branch is the important one; near the inner end this forks, and on the outstanding rock face there is a large cross in the form of a broadsword *(Fig. 6.2)*. Inspection of the sandstone walls of the cave reveals other traces of incisions, as illustrated in *The Book of Arran* when describing a crude and rather fruitless attempt at excavation There were noted the very well drawn outline of a deer, of a serpent, of a man on horseback, of a man with arms upraised (a rather infantile effort), as well as rings and other symbols. Once again, recent vandalism is only too evident, which makes the record in *The Book of Arran* all the more valuable. Some of the carvings may be much later, but the animal outlines suggest a form of art current in the Iron Age. Of considerable interest in the present context is the discovery of what are called "ogham" inscriptions within the cave. These involve a code of letters invented, probably in Ireland, about the time of the introduction of Christianity. The letters are represented by a combination of short horizontal and diagonal notches *(Fig.6.2)* cut along either side of one corner of a slab of stone, or alternatively on either side of a vertical line, as in the King's Cave. The inscriptions normally record a burial and provide no other information, but here the oghams on the cave wall indicate that it was in use in Early Christian times. Unfortunately, the inscriptions are fragmentary and difficult to find in the dim light; as far as the writer is aware, they have not been deciphered.

While we owe so much to the investigators responsible for *The Book of Arran,* one site to which great importance was attached now demands re-interpretation. Balfour first described it seventy years ago as a "cashel", that is, a monastic site of the Early Christian period, and it was marked as such on the older Ordnance Survey maps *(905266)*. It lies in the moor on the south side of the fields of the present farm of Kilpatrick, and is reached by a path signposted on the main road a mile (1600 m.) south of Blackwaterfoot, as leading to "Kilpatrick Dun". White poles mark out the route on its way up to the site. At the top of the hill there are two enclosures, one within the other, the larger of which is surrounded by an overgrown wall of earth and stone slabs for most of the way round, but by a burn on the eastern side. The area is just over two acres and signs of old plough rigs are easily traceable. The inner enclosure, which is roughly circular, adjoins the outer on its northern side; it is about 17 metres across, the size of an Iron Age dun, but the surrounding "wall" is ill-defined. Passing through this "wall" from the outer enclosure is an opening suggestive of an entrance; it is lined on either side by massive slabs on end. Some excavation was attempted in these early days, and a Food Vessel was found in the bank near the entrance. Several very long slabs of stone have been uncovered and Balfour thought he had located a gallery such as occurs in some duns in the thickness of the wall. No finds of domestic rubbish were recorded. Across the burn to the east are three circular enclosures, and two more occur in the moor to the west. These Balfour interpreted as monks' cells, and he regarded the inner oval as the common meeting place in a Celtic monastery.

Much more archaeological knowledge of the Early Christian period is now available, especially for Ireland, and few competent observers can now accept the interpretation placed upon it, though in detail the site has very puzzling features which call for re-excavation. The so-called cells are normal hut-circles of the prehistoric period (monks' cells would have been inside the enclosure). The "gallery" would seem to the writer to be no more than walling where the two enclosures are contiguous. The "entrance" is suggestive of the remains of a chambered tomb and, indeed, the inner enclosure could prove to be the remnants of a cairn. However, in spite of the problem, the site as a whole is well worth a visit, especially on a clear day, when the Shiskine valley and the high peaks beyond provide a memorable setting to Blackwaterfoot.

It might be noted in passing that a cave on the shore reached by a track across the main road from Kilpatrick, is known as the Church Cave. It was, for a short time in the late 18th century, used as a church by part of the congregation of Kilmory, but no connection with the Early Christians has been suggested.

To turn now to the period of the Vikings, a period of several centuries when the history of Western Europe in particular, and much further afield as well, was dominated by the activities of these wanderers from Scandinavia. Many people think of them simply as brutal pirates, but they were great traders and explorers, especially in the later stages of the period. They established trading centres like Dublin, they colonised Iceland and Greenland and found their way far into Russia and southwards to the Mediterranean. The evidence from Arran illustrates their activities in several ways.

The first attack on the monastery of Iona came in 795, and after that they raided the west coast for many years to come. The grave of one of these early Vikings was found at the end of last century while building a house at Millhill, Lamlash. The rusted remains of an iron sword were recovered and the boss of a shield, now preserved in the National Museum. A curious story was told to the writer by the late John Sillars. He said that while digging the foundations of a "back house" on the west side of the burn near the shore road just behind the grave, a pile of about fifty skulls was found, and were subsequently dumped in the bay. The story cannot now be verified, unfortunately. It might, at first sight, suggest a massacre, but the pile may go back to an earlier period, as a cult amongst Celtic peoples in the Iron Age involved an association between springs of water and human skulls; there is a spring nearby at Millhill.

Across the bay at King's Cross Point there is another memorial of a rare type in Britain. While investigating the small circular dun previously described (p.72) before *The Book of Arran* was published, an elongated structure of large stones was found immediately outside to the west *(Fig. 5.5)*. Within, several rivets were discovered as from a boat, and other objects included a coin minted in York about 850, and some burnt bone and charcoal. It appears to represent a cremation burial in a boat of one of these early Vikings. Unfortunately this extraordinarily interesting monument was left open and uncared for, and in time was overgrown. During the last war, a Naval post was established nearby and the area further disfigured. For a time a thick cover of whin at least stopped the damage from visitors unaware of the monument, but now a path literally leads along the length of the boat-shaped enclosure. Fortunately there is a photograph of the excavation in *The Book of Arran*, but now this deplorable neglect has gone so far that little survives in recognisable form, though the dun and the grave would have provided a most interesting feature at King's Cross.

Presumably in later days, colonists came to Arran from Norway, as is attested by a number of Scandinavian place names, for instance, Brodick (the broad bay), Goat Fell and Ormidale. Some of the runes in the cave of St. Molaise on the Holy Island seem to be late, and Mr. Robert McLellan has suggested that they date to the visit of the last fleet from Norway in 1265 when the ships sailed into Lamlash Bay after the battle of Largs. This was, in fact, the last episode of the long period beginning for Scotland at Iona in 795.

In ending this section of the account, it must surely have been obvious that no mention has been made of the living conditions of the vast majority of the population of the island, forming eighty or ninety per cent of the total. After discussing the round houses of the prehistoric period and the forts of the Iron Age, literally nothing can be said about the dwellings of Early Christian times. This is largely true of most of Scotland. Again, very little can be said about the ordinary way of life of the people, their farms and their number. They may well have utilised occasionally the old fortified enclosures, but there is no direct evidence from Arran. In some parts of northern Britain, mainly in Orkney and Shetland, elongated dwellings of the Norse period have been examined, but none are known from Arran. We do not really know just when the round houses of the prehistoric period gave way to the rectangular dwellings of later times. The whole of the Early Christian period has often been called the Dark Ages, and the best hope for clarification must surely lie with the archaeologist rather than in the vague and elusive documentary record. Hardly a beginning has yet been made, however, and new techniques must be developed. Nor does the position change very much when we come to the later Middle Ages. The ordinary people elude us here in Scotland until the documentary evidence begins to throw light on the position in the 17th century.

7
MEDIEVAL CASTLES, CHURCHES & CHAPELS

Castles

Apart from the relatively few Royal castles, the earliest fortifications as introduced by the Normans at the time of Malcolm Canmore and Queen Margaret in the 12th century consisted of a great artificial mound, a motte, surmounted by a wooden tower. One of these is shown on the Bayeux Tapestry at the time of the Battle of Hastings in 1066. Outside there was normally an enclosure for the retainers of the baron, which was known as the bailey. Of this early type, no example has been reported from Arran, though the oldest part of Brodick Castle *(Fig. 7.1)* stands on a natural rocky knoll not altogether unlike a motte; this part of the castle has been shown to belong to the late 13th century. At that period the lay-out would be very different from anything seen there today.

In the 17th century, the old castle was extended westwards by the part which contains what is now called the Dining Room and the Old Library, and a battery was also constructed in the opposite direction to overlook the bay. Still further additions last century gave rise to the whole of the imposing western sector and the outbuildings to the north. After the death of the Duchess of Montrose in 1957, Brodick Castle, its contents and the gardens, were accepted in lieu of death duties by the Treasury, and the National Trust for Scotland accepted responsibility. Further details of the castle and its furnishings are fully described in the official guide, and here it is only necessary to indicate its interest. The magnificent site overlooking Brodick Bay and the famous gardens with their exotic shrubs make this aristocratic home of the Hamilton dukes one of the most attractive to visit in the whole of Scotland.

The castle at Lochranza *(Fig. 7.2)* also stands on a remarkable site

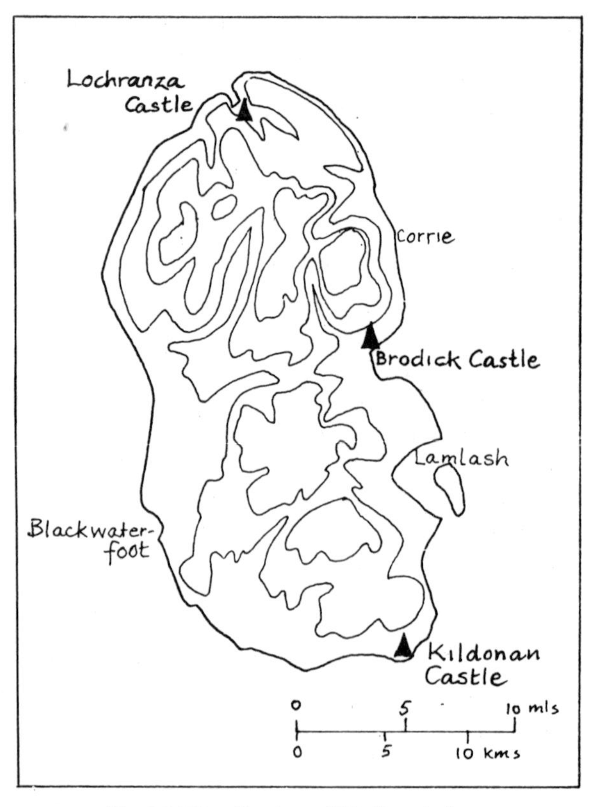

Fig. 7.1 **Distribution of Medieval sites**

on the shingle spit jutting out into the loch and providing an anchorage for small boats behind. Doubtless the main purpose of the castle was to provide a secure home for the baron and his family, and to protect and supervise the traders using the loch as a natural harbour. Comparatively little is known of its original owners, who would appear to have been Menteiths; later it became a Royal castle for a while in the 14th century, before passing to the Montgomeries in the 15th century.

Details of the internal lay-out will be found in Mr. Robert

McLellan's *Ancient Monuments of Arran* (HMSO 1977). Here it is to be noted that the earliest structure on the site, presumably built by the Menteiths, was rather barn-like according to Mr. Stuart Cruden in his book *The Scottish Castle.* It would consist of a hall at the upper level, above a ground floor basement. It seems to have been entered, not as at present on the south side, but on the face away from the sea where traces of blocked-up openings may be readily detected. Not until the

Fig. 7.2 **Lochranza Castle**

16th century did the castle assume its present form of a tower house. Then the new entrance was constructed with the projecting bartizan above as defence against assailants at the door. Also, a tower had been added immediately overlooking the door to the right, so that cross-fire was possible. The hall was still on an upper floor, with service and store rooms in the basement. A long passage which opened off the old entrance of hall-house days, still runs within the thickness of the wall round the north east corner of the castle. It would lead to the top of the tower, which is now badly ruined.

In fact, much of the interior has reached such a stage of decay that it is not easy, without a guide, to visualise the character of the living quarters. Under the Inspectorate of Ancient Monuments, the roofless building has been stabilised, but operations involved much disturbance internally. In general what remains at present dates largely to the 16th century, but enough has survived to convince the experts of a building nearly two centuries earlier. Lochranza Castle may be entered by visitors, who can obtain the key in the village, as directed by the notice.

Kildonan Castle *(Fig 7.3)* at the extreme south east of the island, has a wide view over the sea towards the Ayrshire coast, and southwards around Ailsa Craig. This building was a tower house, but it is so ruinous as to be both highly picturesque and in a highly dangerous state. The Department of the Environment has so many of these tower houses on its hands in Scotland that only selected examples can be stabilised and preserved. Kildonan is described in some detail in the first volume of *The Book of Arran,* but little is known of its owners, or of the date of construction. This gaunt tower was well defended by the cliff on the seaward side, and probably there was a dry ditch by way of protection on the landward side. Unlike Lochranza Castle, the original form is easier to visualise, since the two lower storeys are stone vaulted, and it is possible to infer that the remnant of the uppermost storey also had its stone vault. These heavy stone vaults would need to be supported by very thick walls; they were deemed necessary as defence against fire. Traces of a small courtyard appear to be visible on the western side.

The three Arran castles are now so different in character that it is

Fig. 7.3 **Kildonan Castle**

difficult to think of them as once serving the same purpose, the defence of a Medieval lord, his family and his retainers. The three do provide, however, a very interesting commentary on the variety and different structural history of Scottish castles in general.

Churches and Chapels

At some period before the Reformation, the Island of Arran was divided into two parishes, one with its church at Lamlash, and one at Kilmory. The latter pre-Reformation church was replaced by the modern building in the 18th century, and the only substantial structure of the early period is the ruinous St. Bride's on the sloping ground down from the Clauchland hills. There would be no village of Lamlash when it was built, neither near the church itself, nor on the bay. It is a pleasant setting with a wide view towards the Holy Island, but there is no legend to suggest just why this delectable spot was chosen. Obviously the church would be more generally accessible in a way that the ancient site on the Holy Island was not. Practical considerations may have been dominant when a centre was needed after the parish of Kilbride was established, covering the whole eastern side of the island. A date for the building in the 14th century has been suggested.

Old St. Bride's, now standing in its badly overcrowded graveyard, is in a sorry state. Partly this is because the fabric was long neglected, and the church was finally abandoned when a new building was constructed on a far larger scale in the present village in the 1880s. Also, the interior has been partitioned into three to accommodate burials of the last two centuries, so that the lay-out bears little relation to the original state. The church was a small rectangle, with the entrance on the south side; the remains of three doorways can now be seen, one of them blocked. Three simple windows can also be seen to have existed on this side, and there is another on the opposite north wall. An aumbry is visible on the north wall near the east end, where the mass would be celebrated. The roof appears to have been high pitched, but it is difficult in the present ruinous state to say more of its general character. However, in *The Book of Arran, Vol.II*, there is an illustration of Lamlash Bay from an old print, drawn presumably in the 18th century. It is decidedly fanciful, even in such features as the Holy Island, and yet it is of considerable interest. The little pier and harbour which are known to have been constructed at the time of the famous Duchess Anne, are shown clearly enough near the site of the present

Fig. 7.4 **Carving on east wall of Old St. Bride's Church, Lamlash**

stone pier. Away to the left, amid trees, is what would appear to be the church. The curious point is that there is a steeple or pinnacle shown at the west end. Perhaps the artist just felt that the building would be recognisable as a church if this adornment were added.

In the graveyard a number of carved stones are recorded in *The Book of Arran,* but they are now difficult to find and hard to interpret. The finest was removed from its old site here and re-erected in front of the new church of Kilbride in the village. Approached from the main road, this stone appears badly weathered, and indeed it is a great pity that it was not placed under cover inside the building. The outward face of the large upstanding sandstone slab depicts the spirit of Christ arising from a chalice as at a mass, while below, and now very faint, is a kneeling figure appearing more like a lamb than a suppliant. On the reverse side, facing the church wall, a cross decorated with foliage has been carved. As one of the very few carved stones of the period surviving in Arran, this devotional cross is well worth an examination and badly needs careful preservation. In front of the cross there is a great stone bowl which resembles a Medieval mortar rather than a font. There is a local belief, however, that it was formerly used as a font and that both it and the cross were originally located on the Holy Island; there is no documentary evidence to support this idea.

There is another carved stone of considerable interest which has been built upright into the fabric of the modern St. Molio's church at Shiskine. It is clearly visible at the corner nearest the road and seems to represent the effigy of a prior of Medieval times, rather than an abbot, according to Dr. Ralegh Radford. He commented on the skilful workmanship shown in the carving and suggested that the most likely place of origin, at least for the mason, was the Abbey of Saddell across Kilbrannan Sound. The stone was formerly located at the Clauchan graveyard. Since the first edition of this volume was prepared, no less than three examples of Medieval quern stones have been given to the Museum; unfortunately all are lower stones. They come from Shiskine, but the exact location is not known. These querns are different from those which were in use in the Iron Age. They were smaller in diameter, stood higher, and there was a small hole down which the flour or meal could trickle after grinding *(Fig 7.5)*. The type may have continued in use until later times, but survivals are by no means common.

Observant visitors might notice that other carved stones apparently of a Gothic character, can be seen along the banks of the burn coming down from Catacol Glen, as it crosses the modern fields. They are not Medieval, but come from a recent church, now demolished, which stood on the roadside between Catacol and Lochranza; the foundations of this are clearly visible.

In addition to the main ecclesiastical centres of worship in Lamlash

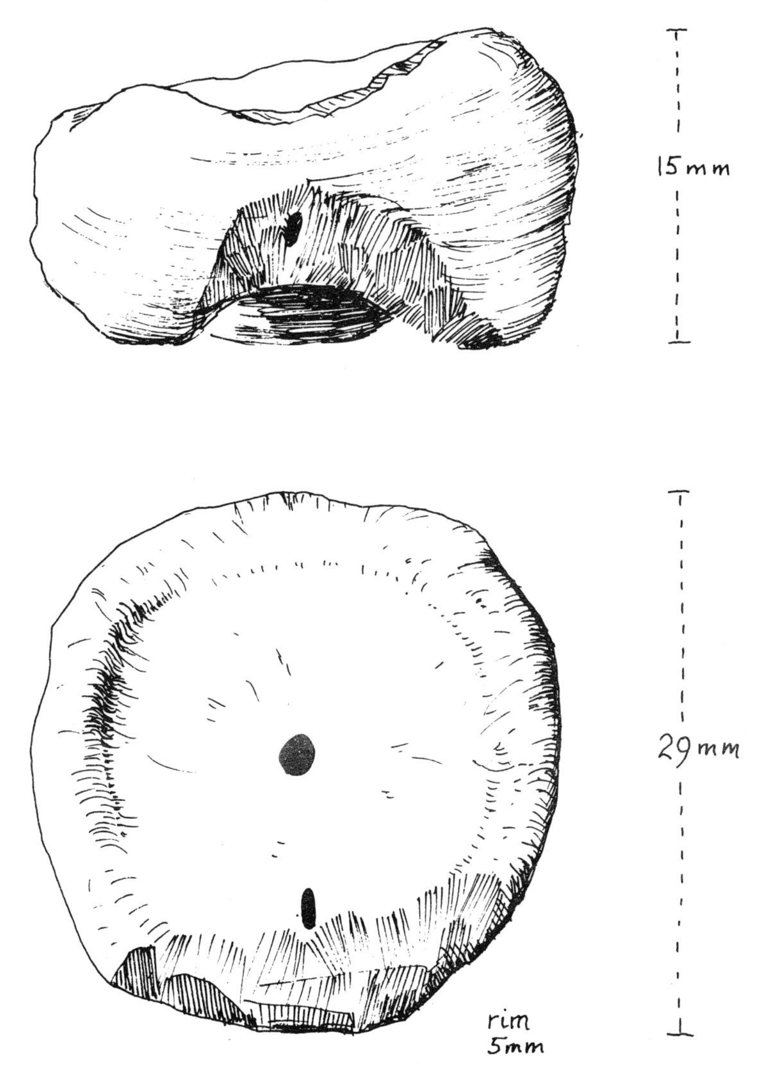

Fig. 7.5 **Side and top of the lower stone of a Medieval Quern from Shiskine**

and Kilmory, there were, in pre-Reformation times, a number of small chapels; once again, details of the sites are to be found in the invaluable *Book of Arran.* These chapels appear to have been no more than some 10 – 12 metres in length and were intended, perhaps, for personal devotions, but particularly to provide a setting for the celebration of masses. Their distribution is of some interest in providing at least a small indication of the areas where the homes of the ordinary people were congregated, though there were no villages in the ordinary sense of the word. Little or nothing remains of most of the sites by which they could be recognised today. At Sannox, a somewhat gross carving of a face has been built into the wall of the graveyard. Rectangular foundations were recorded from Glenashdale, Whiting Bay, where an old graveyard can still be seen. At Kildonan Farm an apse-like structure was unearthed, and several long cists nearby indicate considerable antiquity for the site.

It might be added in passing that the roofless building at Clauchan by the graveyard is relatively late as it was erected in the early 19th century on the site of one a century earlier. The place was chosen for the convenience of the local people in view of the distance from the churches at Kilmory and at Lochranza.

Castles, churches and chapels tell us so very little about the lives of the population in general during Medieval times. The historical records are of the church and aristocracy, of raids and burnings, devastation and feuds. Life during the Middle Ages and well into modern times involved much misery and poverty, but details of the normal living conditions and the form of settlement are almost entirely lacking. When records and archaeological information became available in the late 18th century, the island folk were backward and obviously practising methods developed in a distant past. All that we can do is to project backwards the state of affairs then prevailing, hoping that in the future archaeological research may reveal details which will give a more trustworthy picture of the life in the island over a period of at least eight hundred years, as covered in this short section. Of course changes took place. Undoubtedly the woodlands of prehistoric times were much reduced in area. Any Viking settlers must have merged with the Gaelic speakers and only the place-names remain to tell of their colonisation. Perhaps over the long centuries even of violence and retarded development, population had slowly increased as more land was painfully developed for cultivation. But cut off from the mainland, trade was difficult, and the occasional descents of outsiders, as in Cromwellian times, can have had little permanent influence on island life.

Something, however, is to be learned from the obsolete conditions prevailing when the records became available, a consideration which adds much significance to the period now to be reviewed.

8
AGRICULTURAL CHANGE & THE CLEARANCES

It has now been possible to follow developments in the Island of Arran over a period of seven thousand years, though admittedly with many, and sometimes prolonged, blank periods. Man's irregular and slow alteration of the landscape has made enormous changes since the first hunter-colonists arrived in the Mesolithic period. It is highly probable that only the higher mountains above about a thousand feet remain in anything like a primitive state. And yet the man-made aspect of the environment in the present day fields and woods, the villages and buildings everywhere, and the roads, all represent a development almost entirely of the last two hundred years. The moorlands could be excepted, for they were created very largely from the forests of long ago, but even they are rapidly being planted and a new landscape is being created. It is, of course, not a reversion to the pristine conditions of Post-glacial time, the trees which are being planted are not native and vast stretches of trees of the same age are involved, whereas in ancient times the forest would contain old and young, making for much diversity, unlike the regular timber crop beloved of the modern forester.

The landscape of today has come into being in its main characteristics since a series of remarkable changes which were made in Scotland generally in the late 18th and early 19th centuries, variously referred to by the historians as the Agricultural and Industrial Revolutions, the Improvements and the Highland Clearances *(Clearance sites are shown on Fig. 8.1)*. These are largely a matter for the historians, but we are concerned with them in this account in so far as they throw light on what was being changed from the past, and to some extent with what material remains have survived from the earlier years of these changes.

Here in Arran it may well be astonishing to learn that the renovation

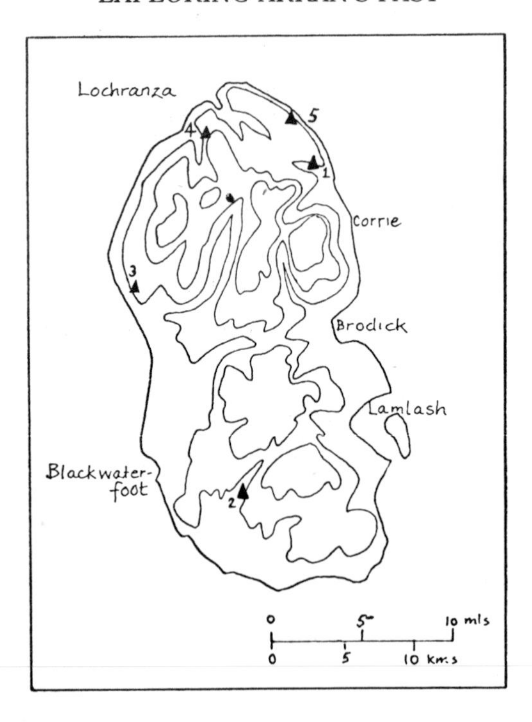

1.	**North Glen Sannox**	*000469*
2.	**Gargadale**	*957262*
3.	**Balliekine**	*871397*
4.	**Old Catacol**	*916490*
5.	**Laggantuine**	*970512*

Fig. 8.1 **Distribution of Clearance sites**

of the old landscape which existed before the Improvements, has left scarcely an inhabited cottage or farm steading which can be dated with any conviction to the period before about 1775: certainly none of the present compact villages were in existence at that time. Admittedly little research has been attempted here on vernacular architecture, but when it appeared that part of the Rosaburn group of buildings where the Museum is located could date to the late 18th century, it was regarded as a very fortunate coincidence. In Arran, however, there are to be found remnants of the old landscape which have survived from pre-Improvement times, and which can be studied and interpreted by the archaeologist and the geographer. Such survivals are rare in Lowland Scotland, but not unusual in the Highlands, reminding us that Arran was very much a part of the latter, in spite of its proximity to the heart of the Lowlands.

Some of the most obvious evidence from the old days is easily seen from the Ross Road which leaves Lamlash for Monamore Glen and Glen Scorrodale *(Fig. 8.2)*. An excursion along this route, which is so well known from the views alone, will serve as an introduction to the Arran of two centuries ago. Not only is it possible to see the unmistakeable traces of an older landscape than the present, but also several sites may be mentioned to link past and present, and with these latter we must begin.

On leaving the main coast road on the southern outskirts of Lamlash for Lagg and Corriecravie, the Ross Road skirts the site on the Monamore Burn of the old corn-mill *(019301)* which relied for power on its water-wheel, but is now a thing of the past. Just a little upstream was the Dye Mill, but both must be mentioned again in a later context (p.120). Away to the right, *(see old map Fig 8.4)* Glenkiln farmhouse rises rather starkly out of the modern fields; here several old "bloomeries" have been located, where iron ore was smelted with charcoal, or perhaps just roasted in preparation for further treatment by the smith himself. Burnt stone, charcoal and traces of slag and ore, perhaps bog iron ore which came from the base of the peat, are the normal indications of such a site. Their age is problematical, but almost certainly they were in use before iron ore was smelted in the mid-18th century at Furnace on Loch Fyne and Bonawe on Loch Etive. A number of these bloomeries have been found in Arran, and since charcoal was the fuel, the industry must have contributed to the depletion of the woodlands.

On the great mass of the Ross hill rising in front, obvious evidence is visible of past activities, as old agricultural operations are much more resistant to obliteration. Running up the hillside in what is now very

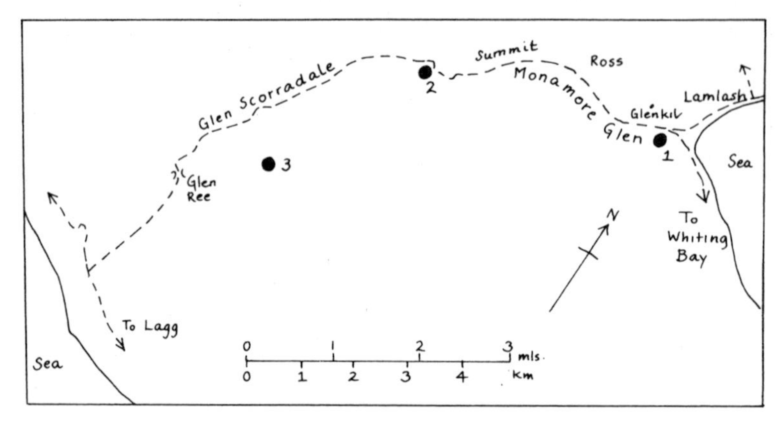

Fig. 8.2 **Excursion route along the Ross Road**
Sites: (1) Old Corn Mill (2) Shieling (3) Gargadale

rough grazing, are a number of low banks amid the bracken, representing a field pattern of the old days before the Improvements. The enclosures can, in some cases, be seen to be traversed by ridges which are, in fact, some 3 – 5 metres across. These "rigs" were made by ploughing the ground so that the soil built up between complementary furrows, to give drainage in the days before tile drains came into use, and to provide a deeper seed bed. Obviously the ground here on the Ross was not only steep, but must also have been poor in plant nutrients; the conclusion to be drawn is that such land of marginal nature would be brought under cultivation only when there was considerable pressure on the island's land resources. A date for the fields and ridges just before the Improvements began seems likely. The shepherd's house standing white and clean where the road begins to rise steeply, is a reminder of the Clearances for sheep which began around 1829.

Climbing the bends on the road as it rises up the Monamore Glen, the wide extent of the forestry plantations becomes visible. One wonders just how much evidence of the old days has been destroyed permanently by the forestry ploughs. In the midst of the trees there is a small group of ruinous buildings which was inhabited within the memory of very old people. It was known as Leacabhille and illustrates the fact that depopulation continued after the Clearances for sheep as such difficult ground passed out of cultivation during the later nineteenth century. At the summit of the road where it begins to drop towards Glen Scorrodale, there is at present a sweep of open moorland. A series of widely spaced parallel ditches show up faintly on the opposite hillside. They have nothing to do with ancient times, and represent comparatively recent attempts at hill drainage. Incidentally, the view from the summit down to the Holy Island is one of the most spectacular in Arran.

Descending the bends beyond the summit, a bridge crossing a burn is soon reached. It provides a useful landmark to find the next site which lies on the more level ground up to the left within the bend of the road. Here in the bracken are old dry-stone foundations representing four somewhat indeterminate structures measuring 5 by 3 metres overall. It is an old shieling site which was in use, probably into last century, in a seasonal movement when the cattle were sent to the hills away from the growing crops in the unfenced fields of those days. This allowed the distant pasture to be utilised and the cattle were tended by some members of the community who slept in these rude huts and took dairy produce down to the main settlement. It was a very old practice in Europe generally, and is still customary in mountain countries such as Norway and Switzerland. It seems to have gone out of use in Lowland Scotland long ago, though place names attest its former usage, but the practice survived into the 19th century in the Highlands and even later in the Western Isles. The younger members of the community enjoyed a spell of comparative freedom during this summer migration, as is reflected in some of the Gaelic shieling songs.

Passing down Glen Scorrodale, evidence of former cultivation becomes readily apparent along the lower slopes which have not been ploughed for a long period. The irregular boundaries of small fields can be seen frequently; they were made in the old days from turf and boulders which had been moved out of the way of the plough.

Sometimes the stones were piled together into broad low heaps and these "clearance cairns" can often be picked out in the old fields, looking not unlike ancient burial cairns. It was from these lower lands that the cattle were taken up to the shieling sites.

Nowadays, only the three farms of Glen Scorrodale, Glen Ree and Bennecarrigan are to be found over the whole length of the glen, some five or six miles (8 – 10 km.) along the Sliddery Water. A list for 1776, however, as given in *The Book of Arran, Vol.II,* includes "Sliddery, Margareoch, Berrican, Corryhainy, Glenscordal, Gargadal, Glenrie, Bennecarrigan". Moreover, it is to be emphasised that each of these was not a single farmhouse, but involved a group of tenants working the land in "run-rig" (to be discussed in more detail later). Reorganisation to make the present sheep farms involved extensive evictions, and the land largely went into permanent grazing after 1825. Two comments may be made in this connection. Even a casual view of the lower slopes of the glen where traces of the former ploughlands can readily be seen, shows that much of the ground was very rough, and only a small fraction has been cultivated in modern times. Then, too, rigs and field boundaries appear in some places where the slopes are so great that soil wash, apart from the sheer difficulty of cultivation, would seem to have been very severe indeed. Notable in this connection is the sharp drop to the burn from the road just above the present bridge at Glen Ree, and again, the slope across the burn as seen from the main road near Bennecarrigan farmhouse. Particularly this cultivation of extremely steep land, and indeed, the rough ground included in the ploughlands of the 18th century, would indicate a problem of over-population in relation to the resources of the island, as they were utilised at that time.

As regards the actual settlements of two hundred years ago, these group farms in run-rig, little remains of the dry-stone walling after depredations for modern field dykes, road making and the buildings of today. Across the Sliddery Water, however, the remnants of one of these settlements can still be seen from the road as it reaches the top of the rise between Glen Scorrodale and Glen Ree, just where a scrubby wood begins to appear immediately below the road. Beyond the

Sliddery there is evidence of former ploughlands in the well marked rigs in the present rough grazing and bracken, still showing green as compared with the moorland above. Near the upper limit of this old arable ground, where the dark moorland begins to rise sharply towards Torr Beag, the remnants of the old settlement of Gargadale can just be detected from the road. There are, in fact, the ruins of some four elongated houses, together with the foundations of a few outbuildings and stack or kail-yards, marked by dry-stone walling. To the right, amongst the rigs, is a mound marking the site of the corn-drying kiln, in which a flue led the warm air from a fireplace outside into a cauldron-shaped hollow lined with stones, over which the corn was dried. Away to the left across a burn, there is a large sheep-fold which spelt the end of the old group farm of Gargadale; even the name has disappeared from the map.

Before leaving the glen and after passing the present farmhouse of Bennecarrigan, it is illuminating to glance at the cultivated fields on the gentle slopes stretching eastwards from Corriecravie. The fields are laid out in a strict rectangular pattern, obviously after a skilled surveyor using a theodolite had been at work. They represent the achievements of the improvers in the period around 1830 in replacing the old irregular fields of earlier times. Again, they link past and present.

The nine mile (14 k.) crossing of the island by the Ross Road has provided many instances where the old landscape may still be traced on the ground, but perhaps better known to Arran people, though less varied, are the vestiges of settlement at the north end of the island where again the ground was cleared of its former inhabitants to make extensive sheep runs.

Coming down from the crest of the hill road known as the Boguillie *(Fig. 8.3)* from Lochranza towards Sannox, a discerning observer would first note away to the right at an elevation of a little below 200 m., a stretch of what is now empty moorland, apart from the deer, but which does, in fact, show traces of activities now almost forgotten. There are square cut depressions here and there in the peat where formerly people used to collect their supplies of winter fuel. It was a hard task, cutting the blocks of peat in the first case, then they had to be left to dry, and finally were carted home to be stacked alongside the house. More spectacular examples are to be seen on Machrie Moor, where the peat cover was deeper and more extensive. Further from the

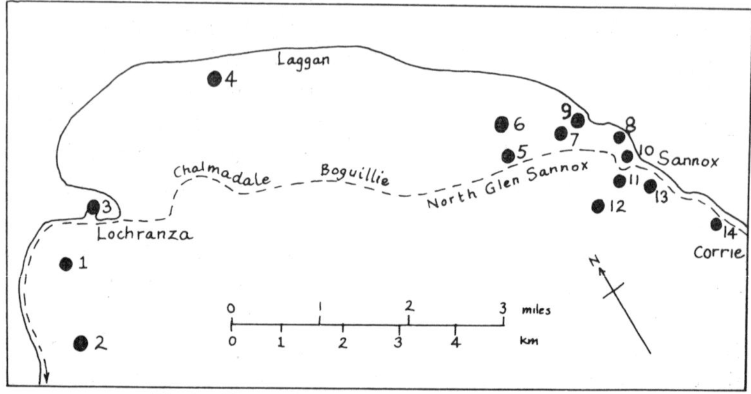

Fig. 8.3 **Excursion route from Lochranza to Corrie**

1. Lochranza Hill fort
2. Old Catacol
3. Lochranza Castle
4. Cock Farm
5. Settlement, Glen Sannox
6. North Sannox hill fort
7. North Sannox Farm
8. Vitrified fort
9. Cairn
10. Church & standing stone
11. Chapel site
12. Old mine workings
13. Chambered tomb
14. Old lime kiln

main road, however, on gently sloping ground rising towards the high peaks of North Arran, the surface of the moor appears unusually smooth, and traces of drainage ditches can be detected. Amazing as it now appears, these high slopes were once under cultivation, even to the end of last century. It is hard to visualise these old cornfields in what is now a mountain environment, and they show to what extent the upper limit of cultivation could be pressed if the incentive were there.

Coming further down the hill, the road crosses the North Sannox burn by a picturesque stone bridge, of no great age, however, and then, after a further quarter of a mile, traces of another pre-Clearance settlement can be picked out in what is now rough grazing on the far side of the burn. Some five ruinous houses, partly hidden by a few birches, are strung out along a terrace rising above the river bank. In addition are two enclosures, as at Gargadale, the whole forming a loose, irregular cluster of dry-stone walling. Rising up the steep slope behind are indications of the old fields on what can now be regarded only as very poor farmland indeed. The old rigs are scarcely traceable, but there are a number of clearance cairns, and still higher, old dykes can be seen, formerly marking the limits of the cornland. There is more than one of these "head dykes", presumably because with growing population, intakes of land were made from time to time to increase the cultivated land.

This particular settlement is relatively well known as the story of the journey of the North Glen Sannox people in 1829 to Megantic County in Quebec has been told in *The Book of Arran, Vol.II.* The Clearances, however, affected the whole glen, and the little group of ruined houses just described was only part of a long straggling settlement which seems to have had its main concentration in the neighbourhood of the present lone farmhouse just above the picnic centre at North Sannox *(010466)*. There is some reason to believe that the small outlying group of buildings higher up the glen represents a late expansion. Traces of several shieling huts can be found in close proximity to the houses, and it seems reasonable to suppose that the ground was once used as a summer shieling. With trampling and dunging by the herds in the vicinity, the ground would become possible ploughland, and in time would see permanent occupation. Subsequently further expansion of the settlement would lead to the successive intakes mentioned above; the very poor land involved shows that pressure of population was becoming acute. The site is, in fact, of particular interest, and the whole slope from the river and the houses to the hill fort on the crest above seem particularly worthy of preservation.

Just as the main road approaches the modern Sannox, there is a most remarkable little church on the left, opposite the golf clubhouse. Occasional services are still held there, and it is well worth a visit owing to its unusual form. One end of the building is the church itself, with the steeple, but continuous with it at the east end is the house which was built for the minister. Subsequently he found this too small for his very large family, and another building was constructed nearby. This tiny Congregational church was built by the people of North Glen Sannox not long before the Clearances. The congregation emigrated more or less together, and on arrival at Megantic County a similar church was constructed, the old acting as the pattern for the new.

The adjacent area to North Glen Sannox at the extreme north end of the island, around the Cock farm and Laggantuine, was affected by the Clearances also. Here is a great hollow in the hills which is well known to walkers as it lies on the route from the picnic centre at North Sannox, passing along the foot of the Fallen Rocks and continuing round to Lochranza. En route, the deserted farmland forms a memorable picture around two groups of buildings now deserted. The two were, in fact, occupied after the Clearances as can be seen by the use of mortar in the stone walls and the less antiquated appearance with chimneys in the gable ends. A number of other Clearance settlements are still recognisable in Arran, as, for instance, at Old Catacol at the entrance to the glen and just within the enclosed land of today; here the numerous ruins of old cottages appear to be particularly small. Another area of exceptional interest is that along the main road below Balliekine *(871397)*; the land was divided into small patches, each belonging to different owners, the various holdings being intermixed. This situation lasted into the 20th century and represents a very late survival of run-rig.

It is now time to look at these ruined settlements of pre-Clearance days in the light of what is known from the written records of the period, without trespassing too far into the province of the economic historian. Why were these old settlements in loose clusters, and how do we know where they were located in the island generally? What did the ruined houses look like when they were inhabited? Why did farmers work the land in run-rig, and why was this co-operative system abandoned? In previous sections of this account it has been said that very little is known for certain as to what Scottish rural life was like in the Medieval period and early modern times. Consequently, all that can be done is to project backwards in time the state of affairs prevailing when the old gave place to the modern. The "old" can be studied in the pre-Clearance settlements whose traces we have been surveying, and in so doing we are probably looking back to much earlier times. Co-operative farming was once widespread in Europe in the Medieval period, and, as time went on, much regional variation developed; the break-down of the old methods occurred at very different times. Here in Arran, the old, now obsolete, persisted long enough to have left evidence for the archaeologist, geographer and the historian, which allows intimate glimpses into what farm life was like before its modern guise was established. The old was abandoned because it was long out of date and new methods of farming had been developed which were being applied all over Scotland. Pressure of population was manifest, and in those days there was little to protect the poor from eviction. Emigration to Canada or work in the new factories and workshops of industrialised Scotland was the only answer for all too many Arran families.

Before proceeding further, it would be well to make two points. So far, the Clearances in Arran have been referred to frequently, but it is to be remembered that total eviction for sheep runs affected only a part of the island, mainly the Monamore-Glen Ree area and the north end. There never was any permanent settlement at the higher elevations which remain open moorland to this day, apart from the forestry plantations. Elsewhere in the island it was the improvements and changes in the organisation of farming which led to widespread disturbance of the population, and emigration. New farms were established on the good ground in place of the old, so that the word "clearance" in this context would give a wrong impression. A second comment is of a very different kind. In the discussion which follows, it must be borne in mind that the evidence concerning the older way of life in the Island of Arran itself is strictly limited, and much information contained in old documents has never been published in detail. Arran must be seen as a part of the South West Highlands in particular, and as part of Scotland as a whole, for which far more evidence is available. However, as far as possible, the discussion will be based on the local material at our disposal.

A series of estate plans of much of the island is of the utmost importance. At the time of the Improvements, many landowners in Scotland employed trained surveyors to prepare detailed plans as a basis for the intended re-organisation. The Dukes of Hamilton were no exception, and employed a surveyor called Bauchop, who worked in the years around 1810. The scale is given in Scots chains, and is approximately 1″ to 300′ or 18″ to our mile (1 : 6,000). This enabled individual buildings to be plotted to scale, even the outbuildings, but the limits of the ploughland are not shown, least of all the individual rigs which were to be superseded anyway.

From the various sheets which cover the estate, that is, most of the island except the north west, it is at once apparent that the large compact villages of today simply did not exist, and that even Brodick and Lamlash had scarcely begun to form. Instead, over the arable parts of the island, there are numerous irregular clusters of buildings of the type described for Gargadale and North Glen Sannox. Some of the clusters were extensive, as, for instance, at Benlister *(Fig. 8.4)* and West Bennan where now there are only two or three farmsteads, but there was no compact nucleus. From the large number of buildings shown, the more productive areas were obviously densely populated. We know from the first census in 1801 that the total for the island was just over 5,000, over a thousand more than at present. It must be remembered, however, that the clusters of buildings shown on Bauchop's plans were, in fact, group farms, for the most part, comprising houses, barns and stables. Moreover, most of these group farms included both the houses of the tenants who were responsible for the rents, and also a number of cottars who provided additional labour and were the poorer members of the community.

The tenants comprising one farm varied considerably in number, from three to a dozen as a general figure, and they combined to maintain the common plough or ploughs, and the draught animals to draw what was, in those days, a heavy cumbersome affair. To each tenant farmer belonged a number of the plough rigs we have noticed as still surviving in recognisable form where cultivation has long ceased.

These rigs were unfenced, and those belonging to any one farmer were scattered amongst the strips of the other tenants; that is the basic meaning of the term "run-rig". As a consequence, no one farmer could live in a block of land which belonged to him personally, so all congregated together to form the characteristic cluster, often referred

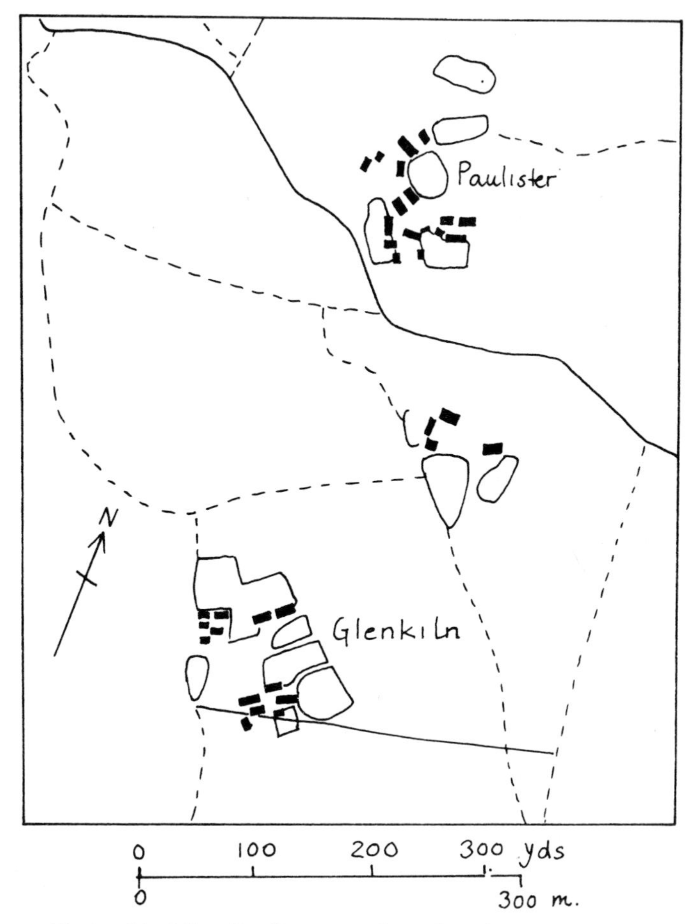

Fig. 8.4 **Glenkiln—Benlister area from Bauchop's map 1809**

to as a clachan. Two types of arable land were recognised. There was the infield, normally the better ground near the houses, which was cultivated every year after being given all the dung available. Then there was the outfield which was cropped in patches, each one for two

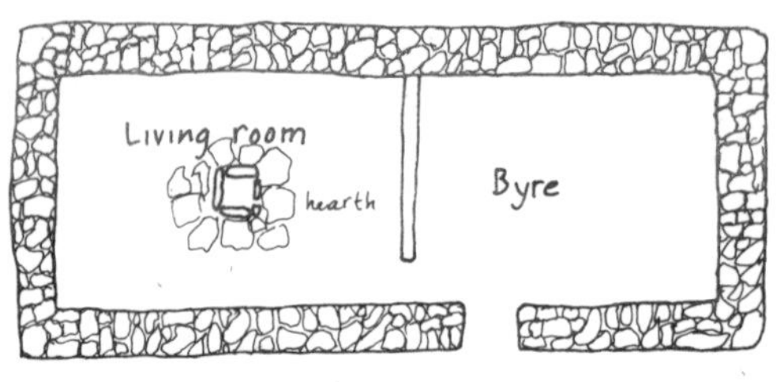

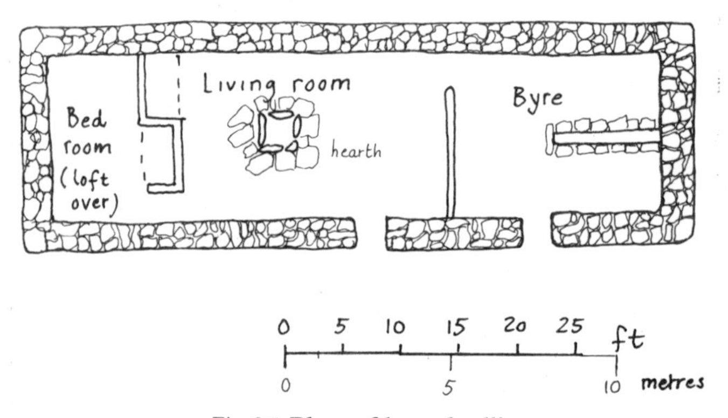

Fig. 8.5 **Plans of byre-dwellings**

or three years, after which it was left to recover its fertility. This latter type of land is often difficult to distinguish from surface appearance alone, but it was usually the rougher ground nearer the head-dyke. Beyond the latter boundary was the open grazing common to the group farm as a whole, and often reaching up into the hills. Here, of course, were the sites of the summer shielings.

The buildings, as shown on the sheets of the estate plans, vary considerably in size. Outstanding are elongated structures which measure as much as 25 m. long by 5 m. wide. They would be the houses of the tenants of the group farms. From descriptions we know that they consisted of a main living room and a byre for the milk cattle in winter, built end to end under the one long roof *(Fig. 8.5)*. There may have been a flimsy partition, but access between the two divisions was open. Often there was a communal doorway for people and cattle alike, leading into the byre. The hearth was in the middle of the earth floor, perhaps with a few flagstones around, and possibly with a canopy-like chimney supported by four posts. At the opposite end from the byre a section of the living room could be separated off by "box-beds", each enclosed by wooden sides, to give a private room for the parents. Over this a floor could be laid, reached by a ladder, where some of the youngsters slept. These "byre-dwellings" in the form of a long-house represent a very old type which archaeologists working in England on the sites of deserted Medieval villages, have traced back to Saxon times, while Norse dwellings in the Northern Isles followed a somewhat similar pattern. Some of the well-known black houses of the Hebrides were built on the same plan, though the structural details set them apart as a rather different group.

The foundations of the ruined houses here in Arran indicate that the walls were built without lime mortar, and it is generally known that, at the time, the superstructure could be of dry-stone, or more commonly, of turf and stone in layers, or even of clay. These walls seem flimsy as they were associated with a heavy roof of heather thatch on a layer of turf, resting on poles. The weight, however, was carried on pairs of couples which were slotted into the long walls *(Fig. 8.6)*, so that the thrust from the roof was downwards, thus avoiding severe lateral pressure on the walling. The inside was normally made wind-proof by a plaster of clay. Other structures in the old clusters comprised the small, and even more primitive, homes of the cottars, the stables and the barns which can sometimes be picked out amid the ruins because a normal pattern was one with two opposing doors, to give a through draught when the grain was being winnowed. Then there were those enclosures mentioned as existing at Gargadale and in North Sannox, which could be gardens or stackyards or pens for stock. It was all a very irregular arrangement, and only when the terrain suggested it, as in North Sannox, was there an alignment of the buildings.

It is hard to visualise these old settlements in place of the trim farm houses, cottages, and the regular fields of Arran today. The houses were low set with their rough walling, with an untidy heather thatch, looking quite unlike the picturesque cottages which survive in considerable numbers in southern England, often of an earlier period. There were few openings in the walls of the dwellings to give light and ventilation; a glass window might appear in the private room off the kitchen, but more normal were wooden shutters. No cottage garden graced the front of these houses, as the livestock roamed freely about the settlement after the corn was gathered in. The peat stack would appear at the gable end, built high at the end of summer to last through the winter months. In general, these buildings in the old group farms could not have lasted for long without reconstruction or rebuilding,

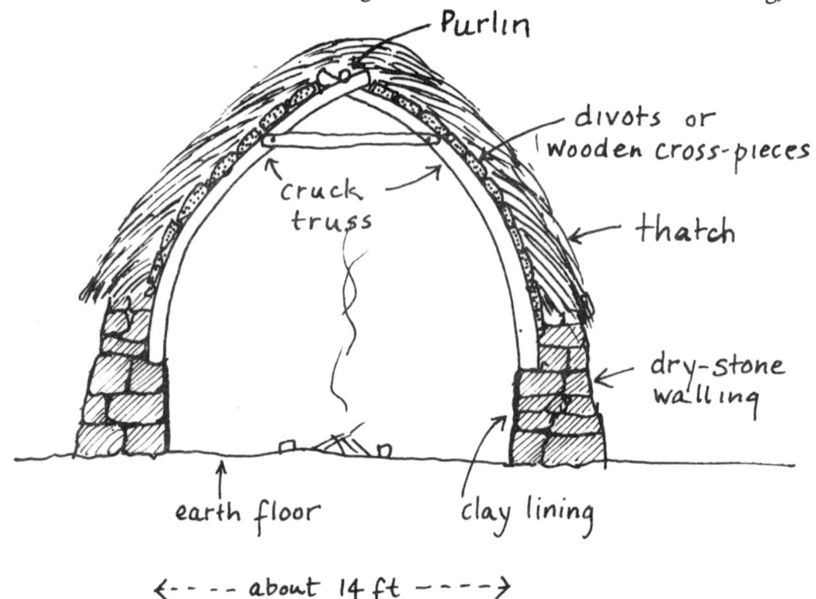

Fig. 8.6. **Section across a cruck trussed house (Fairhurst)**

and that seems to be one reason why so very few examples appear to have survived which are older than the late 18th century. Poor indeed these houses were in terms of material comfort and aesthetic values, and travellers from the south, even in the richer lands of the Lothians, were very outspoken about the wretched housing conditions. The late 18th century was a turning point in Scottish rural history, and the comparative prosperity of a century later represents a very remarkable achievement, especially in what had been the backward and isolated Arran of former times.

9
THE RECENT PAST

A study of the present landscape in Arran is outside the scope of this short account of its archaeology, although we have had very much in mind what the island was like in the past, and what has survived to the present. The word archaeology, in its original sense, means the study of things ancient, but no sudden end can be found for a landscape such as exists here in Arran. The modern interest in Victoriana is a reflection of the fact that we live in a period of hectic change, the obsolete rapidly becomes the antique and the antique, in its turn, excites wonder in so far as it reflects a way of life so different from our own. In Arran, the period of the early 19th century which we have just considered was followed by a remarkable change with the coming of the steamship, and the growth of a tourist industry with its repercussions on the farming community. Another remarkable change occurred with World War I and the coming of the petrol engine and electricity to the island. The young generation of today no longer recalls the fields at harvest time with hay cocks and stooks, nor indeed an Arran which was almost devoid of forestry plantations.

In bringing this story of Arran's development to a close, it seems necessary to discuss some of the structures and features belonging to the period after 1800, which are not yet monuments of the past, but whose form and purpose is no longer obvious. Then, too, there are some interesting survivals into this modern phase whose dating needs a comment because they seem to have an air of antiquity belied by the facts. Obviously a careful selection must be made, and a strong personal element is inevitably involved.

A rather bizarre example to illustrate the general point is the ice house which has just been exhumed a short distance in front of the main door at Brodick Castle. How many people have ever heard of an ice house as distinct from an Eskimo igloo? It is a circular stone-built

Fig. 9.1 **Old cottage at Lochranza, from a painting of 1871**

structure sunk over 3 m. into sloping ground, and is provided with a beautifully domed roof. The only entrance is high up at dome level, but drainage was provided from the floor out to the sloping ground. In the old days of not so long ago, it was packed with sufficient ice to last through the following summer and acted as a freezer. The main use was for ice to make sweets and to cool wine for the benefit of the ducal table. This was an old idea in the Mediterranean, but became popular in Britain during the 18th century. Strange as it may seem, ice could be brought over from Newfoundland as ships' ballast. Of course, modern refrigeration killed the need for such structures, and the existence of one in the Castle grounds after it had been filled in, had almost been forgotten.

Far more important in this general review, however, is the question of what developments took place in house type and settlement form after the rural reorganisation of the early 19th century, and to what extent can the results be seen today. Certainly little has apparently survived of the old group farms; they seem to have been eradicated so thoroughly that, apart from such ruins as those of Gargadale and

North Glen Sannox, it is hard to refer to a single example of a cottage or farmhouse of that period. Fig.9.1 is a drawing of a 19th century farm house at Lochranza. This may seem an unexpected difficulty, and it may well be that the writer's personal information is at fault. The problem of "vernacular architecture" has been but little studied in Scotland generally until very recently, and the excellent *Book of Arran* is strangely silent. Of course, dry stone walling could be concealed by an application of lime mortar, and a slated roof on rafters could replace the old thatch, but not one single example of a cruck-truss holding up the roof of an occupied cottage can so far be given. An unmistakeable section of a cruck at the scarf-joint (normally at the height of the wall head) was noted when an old row of cottages in Lamlash was recently replaced by a modern house. An old building on the roadside at Ballarie, the first to be passed on reaching Lochranza from the Boguillie, may be a survival of a byre dwelling which is known from the old water colour. Any information which might help in this direction would be gladly received at the archive in the Island of Arran Museum.

What do survive still are numbers of old cottages, often as part of a row, and farm out-buildings which, on general grounds, could be attributed to the middle third of last century. These have been built with lime-mortar so that the walls could carry a heavy roof in the modern fashion. There is a model in the Museum of the old Croft House on what is now the Hospital Road at Millhill, Lamlash. The model is based on measurements from the Ordnance Survey 25″ map, and on old photographs, and was most carefully constructed to scale. At the upper end of a continuous row was the dwelling, then the adjoining byre with a separate door, then the barn, and finally a small cottage which could once have been a stable; all were under a thatched roof *(Fig. 9.2)*. Such a structure could easily be converted into a row of small cottages, and one wonders whether this type of elongated farm building could represent some intermediate stage between the traditional byre dwelling and the steadings of today. Most of Arran's houses, large and small, seem to go back no further than the change which occurred later in the century when the tourist trade had

Fig. 9.2 **Croft House, Millhill, Lamlash, from a photograph about 1905**

created a demand for good housing. Whole families began to move down from the mainland, and especially from Glasgow, for the holidays, and the local residents provided good living quarters which they occupied in the winter, but moved into a small back-house or outbuilding to provide rooms for the summer visitors. Perhaps this surmise about an intermediate phase in the development of housing in Arran will prove wrong, and more structures of greater antiquity will be recognised with detailed study of old, and perhaps decrepit, buildings, now used mainly as outhouses.

The Duke's factor saw to it that the old group farms were broken up and replaced by the farms with their boundaries much as they are now, always remembering that the Forestry Commission has taken over wide areas once enclosed. As examples, Aucheleffan and High Cloined have disappeared in the trees and Auchareoch is engulfed. As mentioned earlier, fragmented holdings survived in Balliekine into this century, but that was exceptional. Strangely, however, there are to be seen in the modern landscape in Arran, clusters of modern houses and cottages which are strongly reminiscent of the old settlements in their traditional form. The irregular group of cottages forming such a memorable picture at High Corrie is what is in mind *(Fig. 9.3)*, but

Fig. 9.3 **High Corrie clachan 1980**

others exist at Auchagallon, at Levencorroch, and less obviously elsewhere. It is as though the old custom of group living died hard — or was it an order from the factor's office that new houses should be built on old foundations?

There was a long decline in the resident population of Arran after the census of 1831 when the total had risen to just over 6,000, down to a minimum of just over 3,000 in 1968. During this period of the decline, there were few developments directly related to the industrialisation of southern Scotland, apart from the changes in agriculture and the growth of the tourist industry. At this stage, however, a few words must be said in explanation of various features which catch the eye of even the casual observer. At Corrie there is a quay built of local red sandstone which lies unused to the south of the tiny boat haven in the centre of the village. On this quay lies a mass of sandstone slabs which indicate its former purpose, the export of building stone which was regarded as being of fine quality. It was shipped as far afield as the island of Rhum where it was used to construct the modern castle at Kinloch at the end of the 19th century. Doubtless many buildings of red sandstone in the Clyde coastal area which were built about the same time owe their raw materials to Arran. The quarry is now a great overgrown hollow in the hillside just below High Corrie.

Limestone was also extracted just opposite the boat harbour where the entrance to old workings can be seen from the road at a sharp bend. A little above are two massive limekilns, now long disused. A somewhat similar, quite monumental structure, can be seen in a field below Clauchog farm near Lagg. Apart from the use of lime mortar in building construction, the 19th century saw the use of lime to improve the soil on a scale never before practised by the farming community. The mining of barytes (for barium) has also left its mark on the landscape at Sannox. A heap of spoil near the road just south of the bridge marks the end of the mineral road from the workings, which have left a scar on the hillside above. Then there is to be mentioned the tiny coalfield near the extreme northern tip of the island. It was worked for a while in conjunction with the manufacture of salt from sea water, and traces of the old workings can still be seen, though long since abandoned.

A word must now be said about a subject previously mentioned (p.99) — the industrial use of the Monamore Burn during last century. One of the headwaters drains from the Urie Loch, away in the moor high up to the south of the Ross Road. In the old days, the outlet from the loch was controlled by a sluice regulating the flow downstream. A dam and another sluice a little above the bridge on the Forestry Commission road, could store water and provide an even flow to the mills below. Thence a lade ran along to turn the water-wheel at the Dye Mill. This building stood just behind the present house of that name, and part actually survives, built into the modern garage. The power was needed for a milling process in finishing woven cloth, and water would be needed for dyeing. Another lade ran along to the water-wheel of the old corn-mill which stood by the burn just above the main road from Lamlash. The building itself was an imposing structure, but it was deemed unsafe after the last war and was levelled to the ground. It is interesting to recall in this way that manipulating water supplies was practised long before the advent of hydro-electricity; in fact, much larger and more complex drainage systems than those at Monamore were organised to supply water to the cotton mills at Rothesay and Greenock.

And that must be the final backward look at the landscape of Arran today.

10
VISITING THE SITES: WALKS & EXCURSIONS

Nature's arrangement of the archaeological sites in Arran was never made with a view to easy access and a distribution in neat groupings. The rough ground where so many have survived normally involves strong footwear, and some ability to read the Ordnance Survey 50,000 map of the island is a decided asset. One great advantage has emerged during numerous excursions with archaeologically minded friends, and even with disinterested companions, and that is that many sites occur in places not normally sought out for their own sake, and yet which provide excellent, and often unusual, aspects of the island scenery. So often, too, a visit to some particular monument provides an objective, an incentive to effort not normally made in casual wanderings.

Many of the sites mentioned below are marked on the Ordnance Survey map and a grid reference will normally be provided for each one. In general, the routes suggested have been selected with a view to free access. Occasionally, however, an important monument such as the East Bennan chambered tomb may be mentioned, but no route is given; application for permission to intrude into private ground must be made in each case. Whenever possible, the sites will be described in such a way as to provide a varied group for an excursion, but occasionally one occurs more or less in isolation. In some cases, a route has been discussed in one or other of the previous sections, e.g. "A Pilgrimage to Machrie Moor"; in such cases only a page reference will be given. To avoid frequent hunting back through the text for details, a brief summary will be provided for most of the sites in turn, together with a page reference when appropriate.

SITES AROUND SANNOX

Although the prehistoric sites generally are rare in the north of the island, there are six or seven places deserving a visit within walking distance of Sannox.

Sannox Chambered Tomb *(017448)* is about 200 m. west of the main road just before the first of the houses is reached on the way from Corrie. Turn uphill at the mass of conglomerate, the pebbly rock which abuts on the main road. The chamber is ruinous but easy to find, and the plan of the cairn is discernible: in it is a small cist which may be a later insertion west of the main chamber.

Site of St. Michael's Chapel *(014453)* Turning up the by-road opposite the car park, the site of a burial ground is reached where formerly there was a Pre-Reformation chapel. Built into the wall is a grotesque carving of a human face.

Barytes Mine *(015455)*. Formerly barytes was mined up the hill behind the burial ground where the old workings are still visible. Pieces of the heavy mineral can be picked up readily in the vicinity. A spoil heap alongside the main road just before the bridge marks the end of the old trackway down from the mine.

Old Congregational Church *(017456)*. This quaint church, attached to the manse, lies to the east of the main road just across the bridge. It was built in the early 19th century just before the Clearances.

Vitrified Fort *(017461)*. Turning off the main road beyond the churchyard, there is a dry-stone dyke running up a wooded slope. A rough path leads over the hill through the bracken to the headland on the north side of Sannox Bay. The fort is discussed on p.70 but it is difficult to find as the line of the fortifications is marked only by two very low banks about three metres apart. On the seaward side, the cliff was an adequate defence. There is a fine view across to Bute where the famous vitrified fort of Dunagoil is situated on the nearest point of that island.

Cairn *(014467)*. This lies across the mouth of the North Sannox Burn from the headland of An Cnap on which is set the vitrified fort, but to reach the cairn dry-shod, it is necessary to go back to the main road, proceed towards Lochranza and then turn down the by-road to the picnic centre. The large round cairn, probably of Bronze Age date, lies immediately west of the enclosure round the toilets. In the summer it is badly overgrown with bracken, but several flagstones, in fact, project from the mound which has not been excavated.

North Sannox Clearance Settlement. The straggling settlement of the early 19th century began in the neighbourhood of the present farmhouse *(010467)* where ruined foundations can still be seen. The best preserved section is in the extreme west *(000469)* and is most easily approached by proceeding up the glen to the road bridge and parking ground. The remains of the old cottages and stackyards lie on a terrace above the burn and are partly hidden from the road by a few low trees. It is not easy to visualise the elongated buildings with their thatched roofs from the tumbled remnants of the dry-stone walls. In the winter time it is easy to see traces of the old clearance cairns in what where the open fields above the settlement. Most of the houses seem to have been divided into two main divisions, sometimes with a smaller one at the end, but whether these were byre-dwellings as seems probable, would have to be discovered by excavation.

Iron Age Fort *(002474)*. This fine fort can scarcely be identified from the main road, and is hidden by the steep slope on the way up. It is best approached from a position directly above the settlement houses just described, and maintaining direction uphill as far as is convenient; otherwise it is easy to climb to the wrong summit. The fort utilises a rocky eminence, and it is obvious that the builders carefully utilised the natural features. There are three sections, as though the original had been lengthened at either end. The entrance is from the east. It certainly is an uphill struggle, but the view over the mountains is superb on a clear day.

CORRIE

As far as present knowledge goes, the island seems devoid of ancient sites in the neighbourhood of Corrie and on the eastward facing slopes down from Goat Fell. The old quay for the export of red sandstone is a noteworthy feature to the south of the present boat harbour. Also there are the old limestone workings and the kiln up behind the road in the old part of the village. A short climb up to the picturesque settlement at High Corrie is well worth while, the cottages maintaining something of the traditional cluster of an old clachan.

THE BRODICK AREA

The Castles (p.85) and the **Isle of Arran Museum** (p.137) are, of course, of outstanding interest, but in general the monuments in this fertile bay of lowland are rather unsatisfactory sites from the point of view of the archaeologist. The three large **standing stones** on either side of the drive to the Castle *(005376-007375)* are remarkable specimens of their type, as is a fourth example *(010367)* on the roadside almost opposite the primary school, but little else can be said of them. The **rock carvings in the Stronach Wood** *(003364)* are unique on the island (p.51), but are difficult of access within a plantation. So are both the **chambered tomb at Glenrickard** *(006346)* and the cairn *(012347)* up behind **Mayish.** In view of the considerable number of Bronze Age cists which have been found in addition to the above monuments, it is clear that the area had very considerable importance in the prehistoric period, and it is a pity that something more could not be done to attract public attention to what remains. One cannot help but think, too, that the construction of the Castle and the houses in the area generally have had an adverse effect over the centuries on any loose stone monuments — witness the site of the stone circle at the entrance to Glen Rosa *(002374)*. **Bruce's Castle** *(992339)* away up Glen Cloy completes the survey, but again there is little more of this site, which is presumably an Iron Age dun, than traces of walling over the top of a morainic mound.

However, the recent clearance and display of the **ice-house** in the Castle grounds is a welcome step forward. It is approached by the path from the steps downward directly in front of the main entrance to the building. The circular "house", built of stone with a beautifully domed roof, is set 3 m. down below ground level. It used to be packed with ice to last through the summer, but went out of use with the invention of modern refrigerators.

LAMLASH AREA

Excursion to the Clauchland Hills

The excursion begins at the top of the Brodick hill and could terminate either in Lamlash or Brodick. A stone circle, two chambered tombs, a standing stone and an Iron Age dun are included.

Chambered Tombs and Standing Stone. Follow the track eastwards through the plantation for about ten minutes; the going is very wet after heavy rain. There is a signpost at a fork, where the right turn should be made up to the shoulder of the hill where, in a grassy patch, the chambered tomb of **Dunan Mor** *(027332)* lies just near the track, overlooking Lamlash Bay and the Holy Island. After excavation, the site appears to have been left in a rough state, but the circular cairn is traceable with three separate chambers set around the periphery, now much overgrown. The other chambered tomb, **Dunan Beag** *(026330)* and the standing stone, lie immediately downhill near the lower edge of the plantation, but the ground is deeply furrowed, planted with young trees and badly overgrown with bracken. Amid this vegetation, the long cairn is traceable with difficulty, except in the winter months, and there are two chambers, one at either end.

Returning to the fork and the signpost, a walk to the top of the hills to the east leads eventually to the site of **Dun Fionn** *(047339)* on a knoll at the edge of the high sea-cliff. The Ordnance Survey set a bad example by erecting a triangulation pillar on the monument. The oval enclosure within the low bank is no larger than the outlines of a house of the period, and the defences are almost entirely natural.

On the way downhill towards Brodick, an outcrop of pitchstone occurs just below the path; tools and chips of this glass-like rock may occur on prehistoric sites in Arran.

St. Bride's Pre-Reformation Church site *(032323)*. It is approached by the road to the cemetery in the grounds of which the ruin stands; this road turns off the main road from Brodick just below the golf clubhouse. The building has been sadly neglected (p.90) but the piscina is still visible, and there are several carved stones of antiquarian interest. Do not miss the incongruous carving of a horse in the interior, and note the command to "Fir God" on the outside wall of the east end. The finest stone was a devotional cross (p.91), now moved to stand in front of the modern parish church built of red sandstone, in the centre of the village.

Monamore Chambered Tomb *(016292)*. This was re-excavated in 1961 (p.28) and gives the best idea of a megalithic chamber in the island, as it was left open for public inspection. Both chamber and forecourt are visible but the limits of the cairn are obscure. Turn off the main road south to take the Ross road leading southwest, and after a quarter of a mile (400 m.), there is a car park on the left at the entrance to the Forestry plantations. Follow the track from here uphill for a quarter of an hour, and then turn off into the woods at a low sign marked "Meallach's Grave" on the right. A narrow, twisting path, apt to be very muddy, leads directly on to the cairn.

SITES ALONG THE ROSS ROAD

These are described on p.99. It is remarkable that few traces of prehistoric occupation have been noted all along this route.

ST. MOLIO'S CAVE ON THE HOLY ISLAND

A motor boat plies regularly over to the Holy Island on good days in the summer season, and outside these months special arrangements can be made at the old pier in Lamlash. The normal landing place is near the north end of the island below the old farm house which was used as such until 1938. Note the brown Soay sheep which graze nearby; they are very similar to the sheep of prehistoric times. From the landing stage, turn south following the path along the raised beach which is very clear on this side of the island. The first cave to be passed is of no special interest, and a walk of three quarters of a mile (1200 m,) is necessary before St. Molio's cave is reached at the head of a shallow bay *(060295)*. Note the old crosses on the rock immediately above the cave, now seen with difficulty amid modern initials. Viking runes occur low down on the extreme right. Outside the wire fence to the south is the so-called Judgement Seat, with another curious cross. The possible monastic site may lie near the modern farmhouse, and an old graveyard there was in use until last century. The island now belongs to the Universities' Federation for Animal Welfare which is especially concerned to safeguard wild life. A walk to the topmost point of the island gives remarkable views, but screaming and swooping gulls in the nesting season are distinctly unnerving.

WHITING BAY AREA

The whole stretch of lowland from King's Cross Point up to the present edge of the Forestry plantations seems to have been a favourite locality, and a number of important sites occur in addition to various cist burials which have been reported in the past.

Dun and Viking Grave *(056283)*. The two sites are adjacent at the seaward end of King's Cross Point. This may be reached either along the shore from the northern end of the village, or by the side road leaving the main road at the top of the hill going towards Lamlash. At the latter junction there is a signpost which is misleading in that it calls the dun a Viking Fort, which it is not.

The Dun is circular, about 10 m. across internally, and is ruined to its foundations on the southern side which lies on the top of a ridge of rock, but is upstanding on the down side. The present floor slopes steeply, but originally it would have been made level by a filling of earth. The date of the standing stone nearby is doubtful.

The Viking Grave lies immediately to the west and is marked as a cairn on the Ordnance Survey map; when this was excavated, a boat-shaped hollow was found (p.82) but it was left wide open, and is now sadly damaged as a path runs directly through the grave.

Giants' Graves. The route is signposted on the southern side of the village *(047253)*. The three chambered tombs high up on the hill to the left of Glenashdale *(043247)* are described in the text (p.29).

Glenashdale Iron Age Fort *(031252)* lies in a plantation on the edge of the steep drop down to the glen (p.69). The site can be seen amid the young trees from a point on the Forestry road just above; to reach this, turn up the side road in the village *(046256)*.

Sailors' Graves and Cairn, Largybeg *(054233)*. There is a pleasant walk down from the main road along to Largybeg Point. Just before the Point is reached there is a marked cairn on the edge of the field. On the Point itself are three upright stones within what seem to be the vague traces of an ancient enclosure. The upright stones, known as the Sailors' Graves, are not deeply bedded and are of doubtful age. Just below, to the north, is the site of a boat-builder's yard of last century, traces of which have now vanished.

KILDONAN AREA

There are a number of archaeological sites in the area, but unfortunately most of them are not readily accessible.

Iron Age Forts. Three of these are located at Dippin *(051224)* by the Lodge, Kildonan *(044219)* and on Bennan Head *(998208)*, all of them on the edge of cliffs. They are described earlier (p.73).

Kildonan Castle *(037210)*. This rather dangerous ruin (p.88) is reached easily from the side road down to Kildonan.

East Bennan Chambered Tomb *(994207)*. This monument is well-known to archaeologists, but it lies in farm land (p.29). The actual site can be seen from the main road, and seems to be at the focus of this bay of cultivable land. It can be approached closely by following the farm road from the quarry near the main road, at the top of the hill by Bennan Head.

Dippin Chambered Cairn *(044226)*. The remnants of this chamber lie in a field on the edge of a cart track from the farm.

KILMORY AREA

Passing westwards from Bennan along the main road, the thatched cottage at Shannochie post office is passed *(980213)*. It is the only thatch left on the island, though they were widespread at the beginning of the century.

Carn Ban Chambered Tomb and Aucheleffan Stone Circle. A farm road to Auchareoch turns north from the main road at a point about a mile (1600 m.) east of Lagg *(970214)*. The farm buildings are now almost engulfed in the very extensive plantations. Just to the north a Stone Age tool chipping site was discovered some years ago, and has since been worked over thoroughly. The site of **Carn Ban** *(991262)* is reached by taking the right fork in the Forestry road beyond the farm buildings and proceeding until a ride with a signpost is reached, and the route continues over rough and wet ground to the site. The cairn, the forecourt, and part of one of the two chambers can be inspected. The location is most unusual (p.29) as the cairn slopes up the side of a shallow glen. Returning to Auchareoch, the Forestry road bearing westwards towards the deserted farm of Aucheleffan must be followed for about half a mile (800 m.). The **Aucheleffan Stone Circle** *(978251)* is a "Four-Poster" (p.47) and consists of four small slabs lying close together immediately left of the road, in unplanted ground.

Kilmory Church *(963218)*. This is a comparatively modern building on the site of an older structure, but the Pre-Reformation church may have been at Bennecarrigan, where there is the site of St. Mary's Chapel *(940230)*.

Chambered Tombs, Torrylin and the Limekiln Cairn. The sites of these have both been described earlier (p.32). Torrylin *(955211)* is reached by a farm road leading south from Lagg post office, and is a Guardianship monument. The latter is accessible by another farm road to the left after reaching the top of the hill out of Lagg at Clauchog. It takes its name, the **Limekiln Cairn** *(950212)* from a huge kiln nearby.

Cairns. Several cairns are indicated on the Ordnance Survey map around Clauchog, the largest being near the farm *(950215)* and called "Ossian's Grave".

High Clauchog *(963239)*. This settlement, deserted during the present century, consists of a small group of buildings standing amid what once were the arable fields, now reverted to moor. It can be reached by a farm road which gives place to a rough track. The sites of no less than three turn-tables for a horse engine can be seen in this small settlement, and one rusty engine is still in position.

CORRIECRAVIE AREA

There are two sites in this area, though more might have been expected had much of the lower ground not been under intensive cultivation.

Sliddery Chambered Tomb *(943238)*. This site, which is in a ruinous condition, can be reached by proceeding up the Ross road towards Lamlash, and then turning back when immediately across the bridge over the Sliddery Water, at the picturesque site of the old mill.

Corriecravie Dun *(922233)*. Described in detail above (p.72), the fort is well worth a visit. It is reached by a short walk from the main road where there is a signpost to "Torr a 'Chaisteil". The path in the first few metres is apt to be very muddy in wet weather.

KILPATRICK

The area, with its various monuments, has been mentioned in the text on a number of occasions as there is the so-called 'cashel', Neolithic burials, Bronze Age fields, a cairn, and several good examples of hut-circles. This remarkable site can be reached without much trouble by an uphill walk, with widespread views over the Shiskine valley with its background of hills, and across Kilbrannan Sound. From the side of the road at Kilpatrick *(902268)* where the site is signposted, proceed along the cart track which turns uphill to the right. When open fields are reached, follow the black and white poles into the moor, ascending to the top of the first hill west of the burn. Here is the circular enclosure which has been variously interpreted as a **'cashel'** (Early Christian monastery) or **dun** (p.80). Note that the word cashel on the Ordnance Survey 50,000 sheet is misplaced (the grid reference is 905266); the official description on the metal plate is now out of date. The great slabs formerly regarded as the entrance may well represent the remnants of a chambered tomb (p.32). The larger enclosure to the south and extending down to the burn shows signs of plough ridges which are not ancient.

Two of the **hut-circles** lie about 200 m. westward in the moor, and may be located with careful search, by taking the line from the 'dun' given by an upstanding triangular rock. They appear as low, overgrown banks 6–8 m. across. Three other examples lie across the burn to the east and south east of the dun amid the bracken where the slope begins to rise sharply. These are rather more easily located by means of slabs of stone which show within the enclosing bank. The lines of the **field boundaries** in the vicinity, dating to the Early Bronze Age, are not easy to detect without expert guidance, but the traces of the recent excavations indicate their whereabouts.

The **Early Bronze Age cairn** is on the summit of the spur which rises east of the burn, and just below is another **Bronze Age house site,** the position on a terrace-like feature being shown by markers where upright posts once supported the building.

It is to be hoped that after the extensive excavations which were undertaken here, the various monuments will be displayed in such a way as to make them readily intelligible to the visitor. The whole area is obviously one of exceptional interest. A detailed report on the investigations should prove to be most illuminating.

BLACKWATERFOOT AND MACHRIE AREA

Drumadoon and the King's Cave

Drumadoon *(886293)*. Walk along the shore from Blackwaterfoot as far as the end of the golf course, then turn uphill to the headland, passing through the boundary fence just above the far green. With an old quarry on the right, scramble up the slope, noting the columnar basalt cliff immediately on the left, reminiscent of the formation of Fingal's Cave. Near the top of the slope a straggling line of large stones marks the position of the ancient Iron Age fort (p.66). The single wall ran along the landward side of the headland to enclose an area of twelve acres, the largest fort in the island. The ruin of the wall can be followed without difficulty, appearing as a grass-grown bank with a flattened terrace behind it, i.e. on the upside. A narrow gap may well represent the position of the original entrance. Any houses or shelters were probably built against the wall, and in spite of the numerous hollows over the summit of the headland, no house foundations can be traced; only excavation could reveal them. Within the enclosure there is a standing stone, probably of the Bronze Age, and until fairly recently there was a stone circle below, near Drumadoon Farm. There is a tremendous view over Kilbrannan Sound and Blackwaterfoot. The site of the unfinished fort on Cnoc Ballygown *(920292)*, and p.66, also of large size, is just visible on the hill top due east.

The King's Cave *(884309)*. Passing from the north end of the fort down a steep path, avoiding an electric fence, walk along the raised shoreline at the foot of the sandstone cliffs for just over a mile (1600 m.) to the King's Cave (p.78). Local legend has it that Bruce watched the famous spider here. Two main caves open in the soft rock, one quite shallow, while the other, formerly closed off by an iron grill, runs deeply into the headland. A wait of a good twenty minutes is recommended for the eyes to become accustomed to the dim light; a torch merely adds confusion. On the left on entering, about two m. up on the rounded cave wall, there is a painted ogham. Most striking at first sight is an incision representing either a cross made to sanctify a resort of the heathen, or alternatively, a broadsword. On the walls of the cave in a number of places, are various symbols including deer, serpents, rings, and a curious figure with hands above the head. Leaving the cave, the path northwards now climbs steeply to the cliff top, and a pleasant walk leads to the main road near Machrie post office.

The Stone Circles and Chambered Tombs on Machrie Moor
A day's excursion could continue from the King's Cave route by turning northwards along the main road for about a quarter of a mile (400 m.) to the turning eastwards for Machrie Moor at G.R. 895330. A Pilgrimage to Machrie Moor has been described previously (p.53).

Auchagallon Stone Circle. This can be reached by a short walk up the side road which branches from the main shore road at G.R. 892345. The Auchagallon Circle is signposted and protected as an ancient monument *(893346)*. It is undoubtedly one of the finest sites on the island (p.47), with wide views over to Kintyre and back to Machrie Moor. The large recumbent stone and its 'flankers' are on the road side, the stones diminishing in size to the far side of the central cairn.

Continuing a short distance uphill leads to the present group of buildings clustered together like an old clachan, apparently perpetuating the tradition of the group farm settlements of the 18th century.

The Chambered Tomb, Tormore No.2 *(906324)*. Here again is one of Arran's most impressive monuments (p.32). It is reached in quarter of an hour's walk across the moor from the top of the hill roughly half way between Blackwaterfoot and Machrie, keeping immediately on the north side of the Torbeg boundary fence. The stones of the chamber rise straight out of the moor and the limits of the horned cairn which has been destroyed, can just be followed by bracken growing on the line of the old kerb. The two upright stones near the fence (and the limit of the cairn), suggest an intrusive cist, but are probably natural. The hillocks to the south represent an old moraine, not a series of cairns.

LOCHRANZA AREA

North of Dougarie Lodge the island is rather strangely devoid of ancient sites, almost to Lochranza. Along the roadside below Balliekine *(870397)*, however, are traces of the old run-rig strips which were not finally consolidated until this century.

Iron Age Fort. High up above the Castle on the south side of the loch there is an Iron Age Fort which can be reached by a stiff uphill climb over rough ground most of the way *(927503)*. The single ruined rampart is to be found amidst bracken on the south side of the elongated rocky ridge which forms a local summit. No walling was necessary on the steep northern side. There is a wide view over the loch and away up Loch Fyne, while the Castle below appears in a fresh setting.

Laggantuine and the deserted Cock Farm. These settlements were deserted in the recent past, long after the Clearances. They lie within a spectacular bay of lowland south eastwards from the Cock of Arran. The area can be reached by three routes, all of which have considerable interest, but involve a long walk.

VISITING THE SITES

1. Crossing to the Newton Shore at the head of Lochranza, a right turn after passing above several houses, gives place to a track north eastward, involving a steady climb up to 330 m., and then a sharp descent.
2. Along the Newton Shore, and then uphill, past the Fairy Dell, and a scramble round the Cock.
3. From the picnic site at Sannox *(014467)* passing the Fallen Rocks and Millstone Point, and on to Laggan.

The various buildings are not ancient, but the scene of the deserted farmland is very impressive. Along the shores, westward from Laggan, there are to be seen the vestiges of old mining operations on a small coalfield which was formerly worked here. The coal was used in the manufacture of salt from sea water *(972512)*.

ISLE OF ARRAN MUSEUM

In spite of the interest which was taken in the archaeology and history in preparation for the two volumes of *The Book of Arran*, no museum was established in the island. Material found in excavations or by chance finds either remained in private hands, as for instance the small collection in the Castle, or was sent away to museums in Glasgow or Edinburgh. It was not until about 1965 that a committee of volunteers began to look for a suitable site, mainly with the idea of a small folk museum in mind. In 1975, however, came news that the old smiddy at Rosaburn was for sale on specially low terms. An enlarged committee was called together, and the decision was made to start a museum by preserving the building as near as possible in its working form. A valuable collection of equipment including bellows, anvil and many craft-made tools, was purchased from the last smith. With comparatively little repair the smiddy was opened the following summer for occasional demonstrations of horse shoeing, all on a voluntary basis. Fund raising for an Isle of Arran heritage centre and museum was started in earnest.

The smiddy formed part of a specially attractive site comprising five buildings spaced around a yard which opened directly on to the main road immediately north of Brodick, and on the way to the Castle. The buildings are of various ages, the last being a sandstone coach-house and stables dating to about the middle of last century, while the oldest appears to be a cottage gable-end to the main road, probably going back to the late 18th century. Shaded by horse-chestnut trees on the roadside, the group was apparently the best site Arran could provide for a museum, the other buildings promising room for expansion. Purchase of some of these buildings to avoid undesirable development, as well as for extension from the smiddy, proved necessary at unexpectedly short notice. A semi-detached cottage across the yard from the smiddy, and the large sandstone coach-house and stables were bought in 1977. Both were in desperate need of renovation and modification, but a grant under the Jobs Creation Scheme allowed most of the work to be completed by late 1977, still, however, with a large debt hanging over the Committee. Finally came the purchase of the cottage at the roadside, which, with the smiddy, was perhaps the most desirable part of the complex; it, too, needs a large sum of money for renovation, but meanwhile, at the time of writing, it is being prepared for displays.

The smiddy appears to have been built attached to a still older building which was once a school; there is, therefore, a very long tradition of a community centre at Rosaburn which the Committee is most anxious to develop. The building was used as a smiddy from the middle of last century until 1960. The equipment includes three furnaces, one of which was added so that masons working at the Castle could sharpen their tools. The bellows for one of the furnaces is on view, and there is a large and heavy beam drill for piercing metal. Demonstrations of the smith's craft are arranged when possible during the summer months when the museum is open from May to September.

The four-roomed cottage across the yard has been arranged as an Arran home of the early years of this century. The living room, kitchen and laundry are on the ground floor, while upstairs is a bedroom; on the narrow steep stair a glass panel has been inserted into the wall to show the construction with stone slabs and wooden tie beams. In the space behind the cottage, the old milk-house has been reconditioned and fitted with appropriate equipment of churns, bowls and tools for butter making.

In the sandstone building, the three large stalls have been retained in the old stable. A modification of the roof has allowed a flood of natural light to brighten the displays. The stalls themselves, the large brightly-lit coach-house, and the old harness-room are used for a variety of displays interpreting the island life of the past. Photographs, maps and specimens, with models made at the Arran High School, comprise a geological and an archaeological collection, carrying the story down to the period of the Clearances. Sections on textiles (often with demonstrations on the spinning wheel), island agriculture, photographs of Clyde Steamers, all give variety, and allow of an annual reorganisation to avoid staleness. Outside are agricultural implements along the roadside; adequate protection for these from the weather will have to be provided in the not too distant future. The upper storey of this large sandstone building houses a work room, dark room, and one of the most important parts of the museum, an archive where it is intended to catalogue and store photographs, maps and plans, letters and information generally about life in Arran in the past. A grant from the Carnegie United Kingdom Trust allowed the purchase of equipment for the archive which will pass information to the National Archive in the Museum of Antiquities in Edinburgh.

This heritage centre has been designed and created by its Committee of volunteers to meet the special requirements of the Island of Arran, bearing in mind both the large number of visitors in the summer, and particularly the people of Arran themselves. There is every intention of avoiding static displays continuing from one year to another. Some aspects, for instance, Archaeology, may be more permanent than others, but change generally is essential to keep the interest, especially of the island residents, so that Rosaburn will continue its old tradition as a community centre.

This little book has been written and illustrated primarily with the idea of emphasising the heritage from the past of this Island of Arran which must be regarded in so many ways as quite unique. The

Museum at Rosaburn is now an exciting and invaluable record of conditions in the past and two national awards have already been given in recognition of its achievements.

SOURCES OF ILLUSTRATION DATA

Figs. based on data from published sources

1.2 Land Forms and Geology.

2.3 Forecourt Area, Monamore Chambered Tomb: Mackie, Euan *New excavations on the Monamore chambered Neolithic cairn, Lamlash, Isle of Arran,* Proceedings of the Society of Antiquaries of Scotland, 1963–64, pp. 1–34.

3.16 Stone Circles, Machrie Moor: Roy, A.E., McCrail, N., and Carmichael, R., *A New Survey of the Tormore Circles.* Transactions Glasgow Archaeological Society 1963, New Series, Vol.XV, Part II, pp. 59-67.

8.4 Glenkiln—Benlister area from Bauchop's Map 1809: Bauchop, R., Series of plans of the inhabited parts of Arran 1807-12 (NRA (Scot.) 0331).

From figs. in The Book of Arran

2.4 East Bennan Cairn and Chambers *(Fig. 5)* (Amended by Christopher Smith 1980).

2.9 Dunan Beag Cairn, Lamlash *(Fig. 34).*

3.14 Stone Circle at Auchagallon *(Fig. 59).*

3.15 Stone Circle summit Lamlash—Brodick Road *(Fig. 60).*

5.4 Hill Fort North Glen Sannox *(Fig. 1).*

Data from private sources

9.1 Old Cottage, Lochranza (from a painting of 1871) Original in possession of Mr. & Mrs. Ian McSkimming.

9.2 Croft House, Millhill, Lamlash (from a photograph about 1905) Original in possession of Dr. & Mrs. Horace Fairhurst.

Materials in Isle of Arran Heritage Museum, Brodick

2.1 Mesolithic Flint Scrapers.
2.6 Arrow-head of Pitchstone.
3.2 Flat Bronze Axe-head from Bennan.
3.9 Arrow-head of Flint from Auchencairn.
3.12 Food Vessel from old Deer Park Cist.
5.1 Upper Stone of Quern. Spindle Whorl.

Materials in Kelvingrove Museum, Glasgow

2.2 Neolithic Axe-head.
3.3 Flanged Bronze Axe-head from Ballymeanoch, Argyll.
3.6 Gold Dress Fastener from Whitefarland.
3.7 Gold Lock-ring from Whitefarland.
3.13 Cinerary Urn from Shiskine.

Materials in National Museum of Antiquities of Scotland, Edinburgh.

2.5 Neolithic Bowl from Clachaig.
2.10 Mace-head of Gabbro from Tormore.
2.11 Flint Knives from Tormore.
3.4 Socketed Spear-head from Cloined.
3.5 Gold Armlet from Ormidale.
5.2 Weaving combs from the Crosskirk Broch, Caithness.